Psychology

Learn Influence And Persuasion And
Read Body Language

*(Advanced Nlp Mindset: The New Psychology
Of Success To Skyrocket Your Life And Your
Career)*

Amanda Harvard

Published by **Regina Loviusher**

Amanda Harvard

All Rights Reserved

Psychology: Learn Influence And Persuasion And Read Body Language (Advanced Nlp Mindset: The New Psychology Of Success To Skyrocket Your Life And Your Career)

ISBN 978-1-77485-452-5

All rights reserved. No part of this guide may be reproduced in any form without permission in writing from the publisher except in the case of brief quotations embodied in critical articles or reviews.

Legal & Disclaimer

The information contained in this book is not designed to replace or take the place of any form of medicine or professional medical advice. The information in this book has been provided for educational and entertainment purposes only.

The information contained in this book has been compiled from sources deemed reliable, and it is accurate to the best of the Author's knowledge; however, the Author cannot guarantee its accuracy and validity and cannot be held liable for any errors or omissions. Changes are periodically made to this book. You must consult your doctor or get professional medical advice before using any of the suggested remedies, techniques, or information in this book.

Upon using the information contained in this book, you agree to hold harmless the Author from and against any damages, costs, and expenses, including any legal fees potentially resulting from the application of any of the information provided by this guide. This disclaimer applies to any damages or injury caused by the use and application, whether directly or indirectly, of any advice or information presented, whether for breach of contract, tort, negligence, personal injury, criminal intent, or under any other cause of action.

You agree to accept all risks of using the information presented inside this book. You need to consult a professional medical practitioner in order to ensure you are both able and healthy enough to participate in this program.

Table of Contents

Chapter 1: When Our Psychology Turns Dark 1

Chapter 2: Nlp What Is Neuro Linguistic Programming? 15

Chapter 3: Reverse Psychology 26

Chapter 4: Reading Body Language 35

Chapter 5: Strategies Of Mind Control ... 52

Chapter 6: Manipulation Of Emotions Gaslighting, And How To Be Safe 63

Chapter 7: What Is Dark Nlp? 80

Chapter 8: The Types Of Human Behavior 88

Chapter 9: The Psychological Basis Of Dreams 101

Chapter 10: The 10 Most Effective Techniques Of Dark Psychology 111

Chapter 11: Seduction Using Dark Psychology 122

Chapter 12: Recognizing The Liar 133

Chapter 13: Hypnotization 149

Chapter 14: How To Guard Yourself From Manipulators 158

Chapter 15 The Master Of Your Own Emotions.. 166

CHAPTER 1: WHEN OUR PSYCHOLOGY TURNS DARK

People who are dark can prove a nightmare. If you've been the victim of manipulation by someone, you'll realize that, often you aren't aware that the process is taking place until a moment after. When you consider the techniques these people employ, you can see that they're meant to go unnoticed. Being aware of this kind of behavior will benefit you in numerous ways. This kind of power over others is difficult to grasp If you've never even thought of manipulating other people. Many people don't be aware to perform this type of dark act.

Darkness is a feature of the personality of some people. Some individuals are born with the compassion and empathy that hinders the use of such people. However despite this it isn't always easy to identify the signs when it occurs. We as humans often think that we are good individuals. We believe that people who surround us aren't seeking to harm us or cause grievousness. We believe that those who are around our are trying their best to assist us or, at least, aren't being violent or abusive and have a varying opinion about us.

Of obviously, this isn't the reality. Dark individuals are all around us and must be recognized. In this chapter, we will define and identify the concept of dark psychology to get the understanding we need to keep from being revealed. If we can do this we will be able to be able to accomplish more. We will be able to manage and interact with others more effectively.

Defining Dark Psychology
Dark psychology is different from other areas of psychology. This is particularly the case when looking at the dark, sly actions of

others. If you're looking at the dark side of psychology, specifically you will see the strategies that can be employed to control and influence others. It's a study in manipulation, persuasionand deceit as well as mind control and other methods of trying to control others. It delve into the mind of those who live the most sinister lives, so you are able to begin to comprehend the ways these cruel people think.

The most evil people are generally described as evil. They don't care about other people and are prone to hurting if they have to. They are able to control their surroundings and ensure they can achieve that success. They don't care what they do to other people. They don't even care the opinions of others about them. They just see others as prey and that's the end of the story.

Dark impulses are not at all uncommon among individuals. Many suffer from those disturbing thoughts that linger in the in the back of their minds to urge them to commit a crime destructive or violent. But very only a few can follow through with those thoughts. Very few are able to take on the savagery to do it.

People who choose to engage in those dark thoughts generally have a motivation behind it. generally, it has to be a result of survival instincts. All of us have this instinctual desire to be safe within us. It ensures that we are secure and capable of traversing the world. Humans have three main instincts: sexual desire aggression, self-preservation and aggression.

When it comes down to it there are three main components that are essential to survive.

These survival instincts assist us understand how to live in a state of nature, one without governments or laws that enforce our rules. The instincts we have inside us to safeguard usand are similar to the tiger's instincts hunting its prey. They permit us to hunt with purpose. They let us navigate the world by reducing our own risk and making sure we figure and evaluate every aspect. There are six essential aspectsthat are essential to know about dark psychological research:

1. It is universal and every human has the potential to develop it.
2. It examines how people's thoughts and feelings about their prey-like abilities.
3. It recognizes the spectrum of dark psychology where the behavior of each person is not similar to the dark. Understanding the context is important.
4. The range of the spectrum is determined by the degree of evilness or inhumanity that the perpetrator displays in their actions.
5. Every person has an inherent capacity for predatory, violent behaviours.
6. Understanding of darkness psychology as well as its ideas enable people to manage the impulses that drive them, but also recognize that certain of the actions caused by dark psychology evolved to be a way of

life.

The Dark Triad

Most often, these behavior patterns are most noticeable when you take a look at what is known as the dark triad, a group of individuals that are more aggressive or abusive, or troublesome than others. They are the narcissists psychopaths and the Machiavellians. They are the most manipulative, dark and do not have the compassion that is required to ensure that they do not become detrimental to society.

Society is characterized by compassion and understanding. It is a recognition that different people have feelings and desires that need to be met. These needs are important and should be met for ensuring that everyone and the entire society succeeds and thrives. As a community it is impossible to survive if we don't think about the fact that we need to make sure that our fellow citizens are taken by the right people. In order for society to succeed it is

necessary to have an knowledge of certain behavior.
Certain actions have to be carried out to ensure the survival of the species. But, not all people have the ability to take such actions, and these individuals could pose real dangers.

Narcissists have an absence of empathy, while showing various other symptoms and signs, which can cause problems in the society. They are characterized by grandiosity, self-confidence and self-importance. To people who are narcissists only ones who matter. In their mind the only ones that really pay attention to something are their own. They don't care about what others think of their opinions or how others treat them. This is a huge problem for many, because it indicates that they're not able to communicate correctly with others. People who are struggling with this issue are more focused on getting to their ultimate goal than they care about who should be removed in order for them to accomplish this.

Machiavellianism is described as having a high level of manipulation and the exploitation of other people.
It's intended to accept the lack of morality and the emotional naivete. In general, they don't have a problem viewing individuals as nothing beyond a tool of achieve their goal. They simply desire to achieve what they want and that's it. Hurt feelings don't matter. In simple terms they'll throw ethics away in order to win.

Psychopathy is usually described as an antisocial behavior, which is typically displayed as a result of self-centeredness, impulsivity, callousness and guiltlessness. Psychopaths don't have any moral compass which causes them to feel guilty about harming others. If they can achieve what they want, they're happy. This means that they don't feel uncomfortable with accepting their selfishness as long as it is beneficial to them. Most of the time, they don't play games impulsively, but because they're bored. They aren't concerned about the outcome or how it appears to other people. They just perform it to make a profit.

The three traits of personality are risky. They all show signs of being unpopular and have more neuroticism. But, since psychopaths are those who play with their emotions for pure pleasure over other motives and are are the most risky. Narcissists and machiavellians are the most dangerous They are more concerned with manipulating people when they need to. However, they do not usually make it a point to do it in a sense of humour. They'll do it if they feel it is appropriate and can assist them, but not in the absence of anything to gain.

Why do we use Dark Psychology

If you've been reading and you've been wondering understand why people would want to learn about these dark tendencies and behaviors. There is a possibility that you are confused about the reason why people take the time to engage in these behaviors even if they are not one of the manipulative personality kind. The reason behind it is easy Dark psychology is helpful in many different situations.

Manipulation is all around us. The mass media regularly lies in front of you, and phrasing their messages in the appropriate way to make people doubt themselves or believe in the news stories they pass around. All you need to do is glance at news reports on a regular basis to see significant differences in the way that people talk about themselves, based on the sources. Manipulation is prevalent in politics-- politicians are masters at non-answers or gaslighting people into believing their side of things. Sales professionals who are skilled can apply their strategies with ease because they know how the human brain works and can utilize it to become highly persuasive. They know the best way in a way that puts the person they are selling to in a position to buy something or improve their chances of winning an offer.

Certain people employ manipulative techniques to lure people for fun, while others make use of it to shape people into the perfect companions for themselves. Manipulation is everywhere. Because of that, you'll be required to understand the mechanism behind it.

Be aware that, when you employ these strategies they are not just that dark. If used in the manner the dark trio uses it and in the way that they are, they could be extremely destructive, but there are instances where using these strategies is the most sensible and wise option.

Imagine this scenario: you know someone who isn't going to be able to break up with a violent partner. You may be the cause of the breakup by trying to influence their thoughts or behave. You could slowly instill in their minds thoughts that a breakup will be more beneficial. When you handle the issue correctly it is possible to achieve pretty good results, as well. You can convince people that they would be best off if they left these relationships.

Now imagine that you're an employee of a sales company. You may want to raise your commissions increased but you do not intend to defraud someone in a deliberate manner. It is possible to draw inspiration and influence on the basis of convincing. Technically you're giving someone else an nudge in the direction you would like to convince them to purchase something however, if you're mindful regarding it, then you will be able to accomplish this in a manner that will benefit both parties. You might find that they want something that you are sure will not satisfy their needs. If you speak to them in the right manner you will be able to influence their thought process. You can show your child that you care enough to be aware of what's most beneficial for them. You can persuade them to buy something you believe will be more beneficial for them.

There are a variety of reasons you should be aware of how to influence other people. You'll be able to assist them and demonstrate to them that they could do better than what you believe they can accomplish.

If you pay at what you're doing, you'll be able influence ways in which you interact with people in a positive manner. You can influence them to make actions that help them in ways that you believe will benefit them. The dark side of psychology isn't always bad. Sometimes, we have to influence people so that they are well taken well. However, often people do not admit this. If you are attentive to these things, you will be able to identify these patterns and behaviors to make sure that people are well than you are by your actions.

Chapter 2: Nlp What Is Neuro Linguistic Programming?

Neuro-Linguistic Programming is concerned studying the mind (neuro) as well as language (linguistic) as a systematic method and the scripts which govern the lives for an individual (programming).

It is concerned with the development and understanding of the mind, as well as the complete comprehension of the mind's language with regard to the way it was designed to function and how individual's experiences shape it. It is basically an investigation of the person's perception of reality.

An comprehension of mind's language affects all aspects of one's existence including his interactions with other people to his ability to communicate with clients and friends, to the overall outcome of a person's existence. It's a holistic approach which takes into consideration the soul and body, as well as the past and present of a person to the test.

As Homo sapiens, who are blessed with the capacity to think, it's assumed that our primary purpose is to think or the thought process. NLP is a different approach, but it brings people to the realization that the thought process is not in isolation, since they are the result of one's perception. It is based on perception as real, and it argues that what we believe are shaped by the way we think.

For each person, there are various ways of thinking and understanding reality. What NLP helps with is understanding these diverse representational systems, helping individuals narrow down their strategy. It aids in understanding of three different kinds of thinking patterns, which include:
Visual: covers images and metaphors for visuals.
Auditory Sound (hearing).
Kinesthetic: focuses on the five senses along

with gut-based emotions.

In NLP the person is believed to be in complete control over his thoughts and, ultimately, of his life. In contrast to psychoanalysis, where the primary focus upon "why," NLP presents an approach that is more practical, by focusing on the "how."

How NLP Does It Work

If you're encountering this subject in the beginning, NLP may appear or appear as hypnosis or magic. If someone is in therapy, this topic probes deep into the person's subconscious mind. It examines different layers of beliefs, as well as the patient's perspective or view of reality to identify the earlier childhood events that account for the behavior pattern.

In NLP it is believed that all people have the resources required to make positive changes to their lives. The method used in this article is designed to assist to facilitate the modifications.

Typically the time that NLP can be taught it's done within a pyramidal structure.

However, the most advanced techniques are left for those multi-thousand-dollar seminars. A good way to explain the complexity of the issue is to say that an NLP (as the people who employ NLP are often referred to) constantly pays close focus on the individual they work on or with.

Most of the time, the part of NLPers are therapists and most likely to be good-hearted people. They accomplish their goals by paying close attention to subtle signals like eye movements as well as the flushing of the face and pupils dilation and even subtle nervous antics. It is not difficult to NLP users NLP user to identify the following things quickly:

* The area of the brain that a person is most likely to use.
* A sense (smell sight, smell, etc.).) that is dominant in the brain of a person.
* How the human brain stores and utilizes data (the NLPer can deduce all this from an individual's eye movements).
* If they are lying or inventing information.

Once you are sure that the NLP user has gathered all the information they need then they begin to imitate the person slowly and subtle through not just absorbing their body language but mimicking their behavior and speech in order talking in the same pattern of speech that is designed to target the main senses of the person. They usually mimic social signals that quickly cause someone to relax and appear more open and inviting.

If, for instance, an individual's visual sense is their dominant sense, they will speak an language that is rich in visual metaphors in order to communicate with them. They might say things such as: "do you see what I'm speaking about?" or "why not consider it this way?" For a person who has a stronger ability to hear, they will be addressed using an auditory language, such as "listen at my voice" and "I can sense what you're saying." To build a rapport to establish a rapport, the NLPer mimics the body language as well as the language patterns of the person they are talking to. It is a psychological physical and psychological state an individual is in when they cease to be social. Once they be like another person they're conversing with them. It's like them.

When the NLPer has established the rapport, they'll assume the lead in the interaction by directing it gently and subtle. Due to the fact that they already mirror the other person's behavior and are now able to make subtle adjustments to exert a certain influence on their behavior. Then, they will also incorporate certain similar pattern of speech, leading to questions and a complete section of different techniques.

In this situation the NLPer can tweak and twist the person's body in any direction they prefer. This is only a problem if the other person doesn't know that something is taking place since they believe that everything is organically occurring or they've consented to all things.

It is very difficult to utilize NLP to influence others to behave in a way that is not their own, however it is possible to force someone to respond within their normal the human.

In this instance it is the thing that the NLP user is looking to do is to either provoke or create an anchor. When they're eliciting the person, they employ both speaking and leading to lead the subject to an emotional state such as sadness, for example. If they are able to trigger this emotion, they can follow it up with physical cues, such as touching the shoulder of the other person as an example.

Theoretically, when the NLP user rubs the other person's shoulder, the exact emotion will come back when they repeat the gesture. However, this can only be created by the success of the conditioning of the person who is.

While undergoing NLP therapy, it's possible for the therapist to take an approach that is free of content and the therapist is able to work efficiently without looking critically at the issue or being aware of the issue in any way. This implies that there is a degree of privacy for the patient as the therapist is not required to know about the specific incident occurred or what incident occurred during the time.

In addition, prior to the start of therapy there is a contract which guarantees that the therapist is not able to divulge any details. Therefore, the communication between the therapist and client remains private.

In NLP there is a conviction that there is a need for perfection in humankind's creation So each client is encouraged to understand the ability of the senses and utilize their abilities to address specific issues. In actual fact, NLP also holds the belief that it is feasible for the mind to discover remedies for illnesses and ailments.

The methods employed by NLP are based on an effective, non-invasive therapy that helps clients to discover new methods of dealing with emotional issues like low self-esteem, insufficient self-confidence, fear, or destructive patterns of relationships. It's also a powerful technique for effective grief counseling.

Based on the behavioral science field, that Skinner, Pavlov, and Thorndike created, NLP makes use of the combination of physiology and the subconscious mind to create changes in thought processes and eventually the behaviour of an individual.

The importance of NLP

NLP is essential for the understanding of an individual's being It also assists to determine what a person is. It assists a person to get to the core of their issue and the underlying cause of their personality.

Here are a few more reasons for why NLP is crucial:

It assists people in taking responsibility for events they think they might not be in control of. Through the use of NLP the person can alter the way they feel about events from the past, and gain some control over the future.

It is crucial for individuals to be aware of

body language used by the people in their circle and the people who they plan to conduct business. With NLP you can employ language that is controlled and with intention, and by doing this, it's possible to take control of your own life.

You can't hope to do the same mistake with the same mindset and expect to achieve different outcomes. In the course of an NLP meeting, attention is solely on the client while they are made to the focus. This can be very beneficial since when the client can think of himself or herself as an individual, they can gain greater clarity in the way they interact with others.

It enhances sales, finance performance as well as health, marriage as well as parenting, customer service as well as every other stage of your life. It is due to its role in the overall development of the individual. If a person is healthy the interactions and relationships with others and himself are unified.

It helps you focus on your thoughts, beliefs

and values. It also assists in directing the brain's functions and creating certain habits. It also influences how the behaviors evolve into habits, and how behaviors change into actionsthat result in outcomes.

NLP can be used in a variety of occupations and occupations. It is a crucial instrument for mastering sales as well as personal development experts, self-help and teaching, as well as parenting, communication and other aspects of everyday life.

Chapter 3: Reverse Psychology

The word reverse psychology has a high chance of being noticed. It's probably an unconscious strategy that you've applied to others' behavior. It's a technique to alter the perceptions of others.

In the beginning, the idea was developed by two scientists, Adorno as well as Horkheimer. Both of them have developed the concept of reverse psychology where people react against the other. The idea was coined "reverse psychoanalysis."

Reverse psychology is an apt method used by people to comprehend the things they desire or to achieve their goals. You may have noticed that someone is using it, even if you've never used it before. The reverse psychology phenomenon isn't always immediately discerned. So, knowing what reverse psychology is, how it's used and the reasons behind it is essential. It is essential. At first glance the meaning of opposite psychology isn't clear However, it starts to become apparent with more thorough study. "It could make someone perform a task they might dislike by asking them first to create the opposite, and then encourage people to voice their opinions." According to the Cambridge English Dictionary defines reverse psychology.

Utilizing the reverse strategy is a strategy to obtain the results you desire by insisting or saying that you don't need any thing. Researchers refer to it as self-compliance tactic because your request isn't in line with your desires.

The phrase also acknowledges the fact that psychology is a method of achieving goals. You hide them and ask to accomplish instead of making your intentions clear.

HOW TO IMPROVE PSYCHOLOGY THE MANIPULATION DOES

A reverse concept of reverse psychology. If you approach someone politely or directly, you'd like something done however, you're sure that you will not be able to do it. The goal is to get people to perform actions that they do not want to do, either by lying or insisting that they behave in the opposite manner.

You could tell him "I am not worried making the bedroom my own; since I'm a much better at painting." If you attempt at painting the wife's bedroom room, you can claim. Then he grabs in his hands a paintbrush in preparation or has the brush ready to begin painting.

A lot of children are involved with reverse psychology. Isn't it common for parents to use reverse psychology to inspire their child to do something? You say that you love color with the hope that it will return to its previous state in a matter of minutes. You are a fan of the color. Everyone is exposed to psychological manipulations that are reverse.

A Los Angeles licensed psychologist, therapy expert reverse psychologist, dating expert, and psychologist usually works since people need to have the freedom to use them as per Dr. Jeanette Raymond. "It is easy to believe that because you've pressed or threatened to, embarrassed by it, or you are scared of losing the connection you've done something of your own free will."

Reverse psychology is described as an unorthodox treatment from a psychotherapy perspective. Raymond claims that a media invention is "reverse psychological intervention." A therapist counsels a client in a paradoxical manner, implying that the client is trying to change his behavior.

If a patient is trying to get over the issue the doctor may advise that he stay for an hour each day. The concept is that the person focus on the behavior and the probable causes and realize that this behavior is a choice and therefore controllable.

There's some doubt about whether the doctor's counterintuitive actions are morally acceptable. The patient's issue often involves anxiety or pain but it's not necessarily acceptable to suggest that the patient intentionally create anxiety or fear. The concept of reverse psychology has been a new psychotherapy concept or counterintuitive approach. It could also be viewed as a myth. If, for instance, parents counsel their children to marry the person they love is it a good idea to encourage her to marry? Does this apply to everyone and under every situation?

Experts have told us that the opposite psychology of people, which includes those who are narcissistic and rebellious are more likely to affect people who prefer control. It's true that passive people do the same thing you're asking them to do. So, they don't profit from reverse psychological thinking. Furthermore, instead of studying situations with care, it appears to be more dependent on those who make emotional judgements.

The success of reverse psychology depends more on the type of character rather than on the nature of relationships. It's a powerful tool for people who are struggling from a sense of freedom and individuality as he believes that they can do what the other people do not.

For instance, Julian Assange. In lieu of quitting he continues to fight the actions of these nations to stop his public leaks of information. If he had been ignored or acknowledged for his outstanding job, would things be different?

The majority of us don't attempt to employ reverse psychology to prevent the hacking of sensitive government data. Most of us employ it for very weak motives, such as with our children and partners, or in a workplace.

You've been subjected to many aversions to reality if you have children, or working with children. In the end, children will always do whatever their parents or adults tell them to do. They don't like being given instructions as most adults.

Two kids were told not to play with an object during a specific study. They played with the identical toy in only a few minutes. Similar to the other test the older children were asked to select a picture from a set of five. After the announcement, only one poster posters was at last, accessible.

The children found the non-existent poster very appealing right away. Certain studies suggest that warning labels can make products for children for example, like those on television shows that are violent appealing. Parents may employ reverse psychology to dull the inherent imaginations of their kids. However, they must use it sparingly and in a controlled manner. In the beginning, it will be obvious and stop working If you are using reverse psychology often. Children will begin to see you as manipulative and will lose respect for you. The second point is that you shouldn't apply a negative reverse psychology that is detrimental to your child's self-esteem. Don't inform your child for instance, that you're planning to throw away your bike because he is unable to find out how to move it without scratching it how to get it moved within his garage. Instead, start searching for reverse-psychology techniques that work. Assume that you don't cook the dinner for your child. You can tell her it's okay however, it's time to go to bed as dinner is done.

Most often, teenagers are challenged when they challenge their own opinions, which is commonly called "reverse the psychology." Your 16-year-old daughter can attend an event that may be deemed questionable, and warn her it is impossible to make her avoid the event even when you are aware of apparent dangers like an event with a rave vibe, or a metal concert. You must find out what is most beneficial to her. Again, you do it. You can convince her to take your advice. The issue isn't the freedom to act as the child wants, but instead of what parents would like. It's about encouraging children in a way that is unpleasant to do exactly the wrong thing.

Certain psychologists are against any form

for reverse-psychology. The best way to reward your child when they do something contrary to your expectations is to make him learn not to trust your. You also teach him to know that what you say don't really convey.

Chapter 4: Reading Body Language

Body language refers to the nonverbal messages used to communicate. According to experts the nonverbal signals made an enormous part of our daily communication. From facial expressions to our body movements things we don't speak about can be used to convey a lot of information.
Understanding Body Language and Face Expressions
It is believed that body language could be responsible for as much as 60 up to 65 percent the communication. It is vital to understand body language however it is crucial to pay attention to other signals like the context. In many instances you need to consider signals in a collective manner instead of just focusing on one specific gesture.
Here's what you should look for when trying to read body language.
Expressions of the Face

Consider for a moment how much an individual can communicate with just a smile. Smiles can signify the satisfaction of someone or even happiness. A frown could indicate displeasure or anger. In certain situations our facial expressions could be a sign of our opinions about a specific circumstance. If you claim that you're fine but the expression at your face could suggest otherwise.

Some expressions of feelings that could be expressed through facial expressions are:
Happiness
Sadness
Fear
Confusion
Excited

Anger
Surprise
Disgust
Desire
Contempt

The look on someone's face could help us

decide the degree of trust we have in what they are saying. A study revealed that the most trusted facial expression was raising the eyebrows , and an unintentionally smile. This facial expression, researchers found, signals confidence and friendliness.

Expressions of the face are part of the universal form of body communication. The expressions used to communicate emotion such as sadness, anger and happiness are a common sight across the globe.

The researcher Paul Ekman has found support for the universality of facial expressions that are linked to certain emotions, including joy or anger, fear or surprise.

Researchers have even suggested that we form judgments about the level of intelligence of people from their appearance and expressions. A study showed that people with more narrow faces and prominent noses are more likely to be viewed as intelligent. People with a joyful, happy expressions were also perceived to be smarter than those with angry expressions.

The Eyes

Eyes are often called"the "windows for the mind" because they are capable of communicating a significant quantity of information about what an individual is thinking or feeling. When you are having a conversation with someone else paying attention to eye movements is an innate and vital element of communicating. A few things that you might observe are whether someone is using direct eye contact, shifting their gaze away from their eyes and how often they blink and if the pupils appear dilate.

In evaluating body language, pay close attention to the eye signals:

Eye gaze: If someone stares directly at your eyes during an exchange, it suggests that they're interested the conversation and are paying close attention. But, eye contact that is prolonged may be uncomfortable and uncomfortable. However breaking eye contact or often looking away could suggest that someone is uneasy, distracted or trying to hide the true feelings of their partner. Blinking: It's normal to blink however, you must be aware of whether someone is blinking excessively or not enough. People usually blink more quickly when they are stressed or discomfort. A frequent blink could indicate that someone is trying to control their eye movements. For instance an poker player may blink less often because they are trying to appear uninvolved with the game he played with. Size of pupil: The size of the pupil is a subtle communication signal that's nonverbal. Although light levels in the surrounding environment influence pupil dilation, emotional states can cause minor changes in the size of the pupil. As an example, you may have heard of the expression "bedroom eyes" that refers to the way people look when they're attracted by an individual. Eyes that are dilated could, for instance, suggest that someone is attracted or even excited.

The Mouth

Mouth movements and expressions can also play a role in reading body language. For instance, chewing on the bottom of the lip can be a sign that a person feels anxious anxiety, fear, or unease.

The practice of covering your mouth is an attempt to show politeness when someone is yawning or coughing. However, it could also be a strategy to conceal a look of disapproval. Smiling can be one of the most powerful gestures of body language, however smiles can be read in a variety of ways. A genuine smile could mean however it could also be used to convey an illusion of happiness, sarcasm or even an attitude of cynicism.

When analyzing body communication, pay attention to the following lip and mouth signals:

Purse lips: tightening the lips could indicate distaste or disapproval.

Lip biting: Sometimes, people bit their lip

when they're stressed or anxious or stressed.

The mouth is covered: If people are trying to conceal the emotion or a traumatic experience, they may cover their mouths in order to not show smiles or smiles.

Up or down The slight changes in the shape of the mouth can indicate how one is experiencing. If the mouth appears to be slightly inclined upwards it could mean that the person is cheerful or positive. However an unnaturally slanted mouth could indicate anger, sadness or even a complete smile.

Gestures

Gestures are some of the most clear and simple body signalling techniques. Pointing, waving, and using fingers to show numerical amounts are all popular and simple gestures. Certain gestures could be considered more cultural, for instance, the thumbs-up gesture or peace sign in a different nation could have a different meaning than within the United States. These examples are but some of the most

common gestures and possible meanings:
A fist that is clenched can signify anger in certain situations, or show solidarity in others.

Thumbs up and down are frequently utilized as gestures of acceptance and disapproval.
"Okay" is the "okay" sign, which is made by bringing the index and thumb in a circle, while simultaneously extend the three other fingers, is used to signify "okay" as well as "all correct." In certain parts of Europe however, the same gesture can be used to suggest that you're not. In certain South American countries, the symbol is considered to be a crude gesture.

The V symbol, which is created by lifting the middle and index finger, then separating them to form a V-shape is a symbol of peace or victory in certain nations. The United Kingdom and Australia, the symbol is taken the form of an insult when the palm of the hand is facing the outside.

It is the Arms and Legs

The legs and arms could also be helpful in

transmitting non-verbal signals. A cross-arm gesture can signal defense. The act of crossing legs away from a person could indicate displeasure or discomfort with the individual.

Others subtle signs, like exaggerating the arms may be trying to appear larger or more authoritative, while maintaining the arms close to the body. It could be an attempt to reduce self-importance or to avoid attention.

When you're analyzing body language, be aware of some of the signals that legs and arms may transmit:

Arms crossed could indicate that someone is feeling defenseless, self-protective or closed-off.2

The position of hands on the hips may be a sign that the person is in good shape and in control. It could also be an indication of aggression.

A hand clasped behind one's back could be a sign that someone is anxious, depressed or even angry.

The rapid tapping of fingers or fidgeting could indicate that someone has become bored or impatient or angry.

Legs crossed could indicate that someone is feeling isolated or is in need of privacy.

Posture

How we position our bodies could also function as an important aspect of our body's language. The term "posture" refers to how we position our bodies and the overall physical shape of the individual. The posture of a person can provide a wealth of information on the way a person feels as well as clues about the personality traits, like whether someone is confident or open or submissive.

Being straight and straight for instance, could suggest that someone is paying at what's going on. A body that is in a forward position however it could indicate that someone is uninterested or bored.

If you're trying to understand body language, try to observe the different signals an individual's posture could send.

Open posture means keeping the trunk of your body open and visible. This posture signifies the openness, friendliness and willingness.

Closed posture is when you cover the body's trunk, usually by hunching forward, and keeping legs and arms crossed. This kind of posture could be a sign of unfriendliness, hostility and stress.

Personal Space

Have you ever heard someone speak to their need to have their own space? Have you ever felt get uncomfortable when someone sits just a bit closer to you?

The term"proxemics" refers to the distance between individuals as they interact. As facial expressions and movements can convey a large amount of nonverbal signals as well, so too can the physical space between people.

Here are four different levels of social disconnection that can be observed in various situations:

Intimate distance- between 6 and 18 inches

This degree of physical distance typically indicates a stronger connection or greater ease between people. It typically occurs in intimate interactions like hugging, whispering or touching.

Personal distance- 1.5 up to four feet Physical distance of this kind is usually between people who are close friends. The more close the individuals can be able to stand comfortably while they interact, could be a sign of the degree of intimacy they share in their relationship.

Social distance- 4-12 feet This kind of distance is typically used by those who are friends. With someone you are acquainted with well, like an employee you meet frequently throughout the week, you may feel more comfortable at an extended distance. If you don't have a good relationship with the person like postal delivery drivers, who you only meet once per month and a distance of between 10 and 12 feet might be more comfortable.

Public distance: 12-25 feet: Physical

distance at this point is commonly employed in public speaking scenarios. Presenting a speech before a room full of students or giving a speech in the workplace are examples of these situations.

It is important to keep in mind that the degree of personal distance people require to feel at ease differ from one culture to the next. An example of this is the differences between those from Latin cultures and those of North America. People from Latin countries are more at ease standing close to each other when they interact, while people who are from North America need more personal distance.

Knowing body language can be a huge help in making it easier to communicate with other people and interpret the messages others are trying to communicate.

Although it can be tempting to look at signals in a single step but it is important to examine these nonverbal signals with regard to spoken communication, nonverbal signals, as well as the context. Also, you can concentrate on learning how you can improve your nonverbal communication skills to improve your ability to let people know what you're feeling without ever speaking the word.

Methods to read someone's body Language
1. The crossed arms and legs indicate opposition to your thoughts. The legs and arms constitute physical boundaries that indicate that the other person isn't willing to listen to what you're saying. Even even if they're smiling and engaging in a friendly conversation and their body language is telling the story. Gerard I. Nierenberg and Henry H. Calero videotaped more than 2,000 talks in a book they co-authored on body language and reading it, but not a single one concluded in a deal in the event that one of the parties was sitting with their legs crossed when they were negotiating. The psychologically the crossed arms or legs indicate that someone is emotionally, mentally, and physically isolated from the things in front of them. This isn't intentional

and that's why it's so shocking.

2. Real smiles blur the eyes. When you smile the mouth is able to lie however the eyes cannot. Genuine smiles touch the eyes, stretching the skin and creating eyes that look like crow's-feet. Smiles are often used to conceal the thoughts and feelings they're experiencing So the next time you're trying to determine if someone's smiling is real, search for wrinkles at around their eyes. If they don't appear the smile may be hidden something.

3. The ability to copy your body language is beneficial. Have you had a conversation with someone and noticed that each when you cross or uncross your legs you do the same? Maybe they lean their heads in the same direction that you do when talking? That's a great indicator. Mirroring the body language of another is something we do without thinking about it when we feel a connection with someone else. It's a sign that your conversation is working well and the other person is open towards your

messages. This information can be particularly beneficial when you're in negotiations since it lets you know what the other party thinks about the deal.

4. Posture is the main story. Have you ever watched an individual enter an area, and then immediatelyyou knew that they were in the room? This is mostly due to the body language of the person, which often is characterized by an upright posture, gestures using palms that face downwards as well as open and expansive gestures generally. The brain is wired to associate power with how much space that people use up. Straightening your posture with the shoulders back, is considered a powerful posture; it seems to increase the amount space you can fill. Slouching is, however is an indication of collapsing your form. It appears to be less efficient and exerts less force. A good posture is a sign of respect and builds participation, regardless of whether you're a manager or not.

5. Eyes that aren't telling the truth. The

majority of us likely were raised hearing "Look at me in the eyes when you speak with me!" Our parents were operating on the assumption that it's hard to keep someone's attention even when you're lying and they were correct to a degree. However, this is a common misconception that people often keep eye contact to conceal the truth the lie is being told. The problem is that a lot people overcompensate and maintain eye contact for so long that it's uncomfortable. In the an average Americans keep eye contact between between seven and ten seconds. That's more time while listening to talk than when we're listening. If you're talking with someone whose stare is making you squirm--especially if they're very still and unblinking--something is up, and they might be lying you.

Chapter 5: Strategies Of Mind Control

It's interesting to know how control is in use for a long time and is not the only or most insignificant concept. Knowing what the specifics of influence actually is can be crucial, in order to help you in managing it. In this article, we look at the brain's science of control. This lets us see how it might play out throughout our life. This will also assist you identify those who are trying to take control of you. It's not just about those who seek to dominate. In the event that we aren't familiar of what's going on to us, we might be prompted to behave in ways which are not recognizable to our normal behavior and character. Discover how trade could influence customers to purchase their goods and ventures. Knowing these strategies will assist in the management of the persuasive ability.

We are accustomed to the notion that we're people who can make rational decisions. In the course of our lives it is not always the case that we have total control and do not always understand this. As children we are affected by our parents and don't have any control over the way we are educated. When we enter the schooling environment We are also controlled. Teachers will inform us the acceptable practices and expectations from us in the public sphere. As adults, we are lured by legislators who want to gain a large number of votes. Many are enticed to vote to vote in favor of a group because of what they promise in the near future no matter if they really believe in their methods. These lawmakers have power and their decisions will affect our lives. Are we able to claim that we're in complete in charge of the events that happen to us or could we simply say that we are just influenced by the people who have a complete understanding of every single trick of influence?

Persuasive Language

The form of speech in which every image

tells an event is evident. Words are more impressive in the way they affect and assist us, sometimes even in the direction of control. How many times have you been drawn to a spirited speaker, whose enthralling thoughts entices you into it? Words can be a powerful force when we're completely lost in a book that is truly amazing. The skill of words is so powerful in influencing us to accept the truth, even the moment our eyes are able to guide us. Correspondence can be a huge resource, especially when it is used to motivate people to accomplish their goals.

Sales and marketing professionals make use of language to convince us that their product is what we want. With words like "reasonable," "easy to use," "safe," "enjoyable," "time-saving," "guaranteed to last." Notice how each one of these phrases leads us to believe they are confident about their product.

* Politicians may use words like "we" to make you feel included as part of their own

reality, or "us" to make you to feel part of a larger group. These are all strategies of correspondence to make us feel part of the group, and consequently crucial.

Menaces employ language in conjunction with brutal conduct to achieve their narrow-minded goals.

The criminal hunters similar to psychopaths, mental cases, and narcissists are typically those who have become adept at using appealing words. This can be a method to learn their particular style and control the behavior of someone else.

Techniques employed to Control Mind Mind Control

The present-day method of mind control is imaginative and mental. Studies show that through identifying the techniques to control the mind and removing the negative effects, they can be reduced or eliminated in any case to make mind control public and declaration. It is becoming increasingly difficult to fight the actual issues, which the military-machine complex is constantly trying to make and improving.

1. Education: This is the most obviousthing, but the other parts are most difficult to grasp. It's been a despot's goal to "educate" generally receptive youths and, as such, it was a key component of Communist and Fascist extreme systems since the very beginning. There is no one more successful in revealing the motivations of the present-day governing system more than Charlotte Iserbyt. One can begin an studying this subject with her work in an absolutely free PDF. The Deliberate Dumbing Down of America uncovering the role of Globalist foundations in constructing an idealized future designed to produce submissive machines, governed by a highly educated and carefully selected class.

2. Promotions and advertising: Edward Bernays has been mentioned as the creator of the culture of consumption that was designed to focus on people's mental self-image (or lack of it) to transform a desire into a desire. It was originally planned for

items such as cigarettes, as an example. However, Bernays also noted in his 1928 book, Propaganda, that "deliberate public exposure is the arm of the unalterable government." This is evident clearly in the top-level police state, as well as the creation of local nark culture that is encased in the pseudo-excited War on Terror. The expanding association of media has allowed the whole corporate design to join with the state and is currently utilizing an option of proclamation. Print, film, media television, and even connections news will now have the possibility of working seamlessly to form a message that seems to be in the realm of truth because it originates with a large number of sources at once. As one is able to move towards becoming more sensitive to perceive the basic "message," one will observe this etching becoming all-finished. This isn't just to measure the subconscious education.

3. Prescient programming: Many doubt that the judicious writing of PC programs is true.

Programming that is prescient has its roots in a predominantly elitist Hollywood in which the large screen provides a powerful view of the direction society is heading. Simply look back at movies and books you believed were unreliable, as well as "science science fiction" and look at the present society. If you want a quick and slick analysis of unambiguous models Vigilant Citizen is a amazing resource that is sure to inspire you to look at "delight" in a completely singular way.

4. Politics, sports or religion. A few people may be averse to religion, or even authority issues, created using sports as a method to control their mind. The fundamental idea is the same across all of them the game: to disconnect and win. The structures are simple in that they block the natural desire of individuals to show their determination, and teach people to create groups that are bowed to control and win. The sport has consistently performed function as a major redirection that represses natural

tendencies into a smaller-scale event which , in contemporary America has been seen in a way that is absurd, where tensions are triggered by an individual who is a VIP in their city, however, for the most fundamental human problems such as the possibility is dismissed as trivial.

5. Water, food as well as air, additives harmful substances, and other food items can alter the mind science of create a sense of the person feel more relaxed and calm. The presence of fluoride in drinking water has been proven to reduce the IQ. The aspartame compound or MSG are excitotoxins that trigger neurotransmitters, until they shut the bucket, and the simple acceptance of the food products that are laced with these poisons in all aspects is resulting in a large population that needs cooperation and motivation to live an active life style. Most of the world's frontline workers are perfectly prepared to be uninvolved in the response and acceptance of the tyrant as supreme.

6. The effects of medication: we could compare it to any addictive substance however, the function of the brain regulators is to ensure that you are exposed to some kind of. One of the most important aspects of the mind control that is at the forefront of motivation is psychiatry. It seeks to define all people as a result of their condition and not their potential. The concept was outlined in books like Brave New World. Today, it has been taken to extensively help limits as restorative mistreatment has gotten hold where about everyone has a kind of disarray--particularly the people who question authority. Nerve sedates are used within the military has resulted in massive numbers of suicides. For the sake of completeness the most prominent prescription state at present includes more than percent of U.S. adolescents on mind-desensitizing medication.

7. Military testing: There's an extensive history of the military as a demonstration

grounds of mind-control. The military personality is the most flexible as those who are seeking the afterlife in the military , all things contemplated are in tune with the concepts of control, movement, and the need for unquestioned acceptance of the mission. To accommodate the increasing number of military personnel examining their impacts, a regular report from DARPA highlighted its game plans for trans cranial psyche controls defenses for the head that keep them focused.

8. Electromagnetic Territory: An electromagnetic soup covers us all being energized by the modern day devices of relaxation that have discovered to influence mind work. As a proof of what's possible one scientist is working with an "divine being head defense" to trigger dreams by altering the field of electromagnetic radiation in the brain. Our brain's high-level soup is actively sprayed by mind-altering waves. The variety of potential outcomes like telephone towers are currently available

to the character regulator for more precise intervention.

Control of the mind is much more prevalent than people imagine. It's not easy to recognize due to its delicate nature. It often occurs in what is regarded as normal conditions, such as the media, education, religious shows, commercials and numerous other things. The cults and their leaders use the power of mind to manipulate their followers and influence their actions. It's not easy to recognize mind control. But, once one recognizes that it is happening, one can take out and begin again.

CHAPTER 6: MANIPULATION OF EMOTIONS GASLIGHTING, AND HOW TO BE SAFE

Human emotions can grab hold of a person's life and alter their actions, often superseding the logic of rationality. People are compelled to react in a way that is triggered by emotions such as love, anger and jealousy. Sometimes, the actions that we take are not possible to reverse and an endless collection of stories are used as warnings against the temptation to let your emotions flow and letting them run away before you think things through.

In terms of the power of influence and controlling, manipulation of emotions is among the most powerful tools the practitioner of dark psychology may utilize, since people who give in to emotions is prone to abandon reason and logic in the interest of satisfying the emotions that consume them. For instance, a person who is so committed to an individual that they'll abandon any other relationship for the purpose of retaining the person she is with is an excellent illustration of someone who is into the trap of manipulative emotions. A genuine and caring person would request a girlfriend or spouse to end the relationship that is positive with their family members, but the fact that she does this upon request of her partner indicate that her affection and dependence on this partner is beyond the realm of the rational thinking that could lead the person to take a different decision for her own interests.

To build emotional dependency, it requires consistency and perseverance. When the person has reached the desired outcome, he'll begin by imagining the ideal partner, as we did in the previous chapter. The aim is to create an ideal partner that is kind, compassionate, selfless, and lavishes her with praise and gifts as well as his time. Whatever she needs she wants, he will give it all to her very best of his abilities. This can create a sexy relationship with your partner and she'll be doing all she can to satisfy him as a result.

The consequence of this type of relationship and addiction results in that, when the manipulator begins moving away from the victim, she will be in a state of panic about being deprived of the attention she's used to. It's the following phase in the game where the manipulator plays to her feelings of attachment. He may make excuses for needing to get away or create a space between them, however, it is important to keep the communication, possibly through texts or emails so that there's an attachment, and she doesn't choose to cut off communication completely. The length of time he takes off is dependent on the circumstance however, eventually it will be back to her side and give her an enormous amount of what she's been longing for, and all of the feelings will come back to her.

The next step is to make a stronger connection between them in a way. It is likely that he will be able to return to the level of affection he showed in the past, however it is vital to continue trying to create a stronger bond in the same way that natural relationships grow stronger through time and perseverance and overcoming difficult times. He will talk to her and share any emotions or turmoil he's experiencing that are causing him to pull away. This will create a sense of empathy in his companion, who she will be able to hold onto when he next leaves, which is likely to occur soon.

This pattern is repeated but not always in a way that is obvious. There is a possibility to withdraw physically and not emotionally as well, which can make it feel like you aren't part of the emotional connection that the couple typically had.

The method will be different and in different degrees depending on the person who is involved and the outcome can be very nefarious. Another aspect of manipulative of the emotional dependence is that after the addictive addiction has been created the manipulator may begin to solicit things from his companion in exchange to show his love, even although it's not a direct exchange. The requests are made in a heartfelt dialogue and the person being targeted is then gently guided to an understanding that they needs to perform this in order to please her partner or sacrifice that in order to win him back or whatever. Maybe he creates a competition scenario in which he declares that he's trying to squelch his desire for another woman, and if she did one thing or another or devoted her time to whatever job they decide to do, then she might be able to win him back for an excellent price. This is just one example of many options that pop to you once the manipulator has his victim at his mercy.

Gaslighting

In the process of removing ourselves from manipulation of emotions a little however, there is a second method that is used in dark psychology that can cause debilitating effects on the person who is. Although establishing an emotional dependence prior to using a gaslighting technique could make the results more intense, it's not required for the independent mental damage that comes after a successful gaslighting effort.

Gaslighting is a successful technique that can be done either intentionally or accidentally. We'll first have a better understanding of what exactly gaslighting means before looking at some instances of what occurs.

Gaslighting is a repercussion in the course of time when someone makes the victim to reevaluate his/her life by repeatedly denying the reality that he/she is experiencing. A victim may initially try to fight to defend themselves with violence, but in time, as long as the actions continue to follow identical to the abuse, the victim could be confused and disregarded as they begin to question their own self-worth even though they'd been so certain of the reality they had witnessed. A mother, for instance, is known to be a harsh and abusive mother to her daughter, but then the next day , when her daughter is able to speak out about her actions she denies that she was involved in any of the incidents. The child may cry, shout and swear, and attempt every effort to convince her mother to admit the hurt she's caused her, but nothing is successful. The abuse is not stopped and the denial persists without the mother letting one inch. In time, this can have an extremely psychological and emotional impact that can be endured as a lifetime burden.

It is impossible to underestimate the effect of emotional pressure. When a victim is emotionalally broken doors open up to manipulate methods. Similar to the narcissist model in which he lavishes love and before fading away from the gaslighting victim, the gaslighting victim is likely to begin to feel a urgent desire for the manipulator to acknowledge the actions of his/her manipulator but this never happens.

As previously mentioned, gaslighting may be unintentionally the fault of the manipulator once they have fallen into a pattern of denial. If he denies wrongdoings and then is able to forget what he has done and creates an insurmountable wall in the face of the facts. Although the perpetrator could prove beyond doubt what transpired the manipulator will persist in denial, which causes the victim to feel a great deal of anger and anxiety for the victim.

How to Safeguard Yourself

When gaslighting happens in the child's

development, it can be difficult for the child who is not protected to defend herself, since the gaslighting will usually be emanating from someone with control or a caregiver who the child relies on. These tales are tragic and the trauma and abuse caused by childhood trauma can be long-lasting and serious in their psychological consequences. As we age we realize that the world isn't filled with sincere and well-meaning people, and we are taught to be wary of who we give our details to. The degree of trust we keep from other people varies based on individual characteristics, however, the majority of us have discovered the dangers associated in putting our trust in strangers. Anyone who has experienced having their credit card number stolen or had their vehicle broken into understands that these things happen due to the whim of a chance, as well as out of motives. People we love have an enormous amount of influence when it comes to manipulating because love and trust are present and ready to be exploited if they choose to.

One of the toughest lessons to comprehend when it comes to protecting yourself from manipulative tactics is that it's not always easy to know the people we meet and what's happening within their lives, regardless when they're family members or a partner or a close acquaintance. There are many stories that we can give as examples which include spouses who are able to cheat their spouse cash, or become physically and verbally abusive or have a distinct life away from the spouse's eyes. If you're determined to protect yourself, or suspect that you be aware of someone who is gaslighting on someone you love be sure to consider the warning signs you're receiving in relation to how well they line to someone else who is employing these methods of manipulation.

A prime indications for trouble occurs when one's mood is erratic without obvious reason. It could be that he is positive and cheerful one moment and then sank into depression and sombreness the next. If there's no clear reason why this might be happening, try talking to them in order to determine what's happening however they will shut down and won't even engage in conversation.

It could be a sign that something is unusual or wrong in his mental health. It could be a sign of a mood disorder, or it could be brewing a malicious intent. If that's the case, and you may not be aware of exactly what's happening It is advisable to observe the behavior of the person and keep track of any other changes or changes that are becoming worse. It is possible that the person will require medical attention for a mood disorder as well as other options.

Another indication to use as a red alert is the moment someone says or does something that he's clearly embarrassed aboutand then is able to forget or even deny that he's ever done such a thing. It could be a quick reaction that develops as time passes, resulting in the public being shocked and concerned. Denial is a very strong defence mechanism to deal with emotional discomfort and extreme stress. If someone is convinced that they have discovered a way to get out of the pain, they might opt to follow the path of denial since they can block out their reality and create a brand new reality in which these issues do not exist. It's like a psychological cocoon which people are trapped into to alleviate their emotional suffering. There are many who go through an emotional state of grief that is characterized by denial of the events that took place. It could be that there was a sudden deaththat was unexpected and the pain and shock are too much all at one time in the moment of discovering. It is common that the brain will immediately block out the truth and pretend that no thing is actually happening.

It's perfectly normal to experience this phase, so long as the individual eventually gets over it and continues the grieving process that is a normal reaction to loss.

Changes in personality, denial and eventually, an escalating pattern of emotional outbursts and self-control issues followed by, if it's not completely denial, then playing down his actions until the point where he thinks the behavior was not so terrible. A spouse, for instance, may have been drunk and then said something he regrets to his partner and then, immediately following or when the wife mentions it then he'll downplay the whole incident, claiming to him that he just used a vulgar term only once or twice. However, he did not say any of all the things. You're making it up. the story up, he'd never do this, etc. If he's fallen into a pattern of drinking alcohol and tends to be angry, it could turn into a destructive routine if the wife doesn't figure things out and gets immediate assistance or get him rid of him.

When any of the above behavior indicators appear within your daily life it's advised to begin paying attention. It's recommended to attempt to discuss the issue and identify the issue before it becomes out of control. If someone's behavior begins to impact you in a negative manner it is important to know what's happening and why you're not going to allow the behavior. The person has a sense, assuming cognitive ability that what they are doing will hurt you in some way, and realizes that if it persists, you'll be forced to quit and not be around to deal with this anymore. In the event of a seriousness of the situation the person you're trying to communicate with might break down and apologize when they realize how much his actions are hurting others. Or, the person may immediately begin with the mentioned methods of manipulation to keep you within his world. If the hurtful behavior or abuse persists, you should act, whether to seek help for the person or get them out of the situation. If you observe the beginning of a pattern, and you see the cycle of abuse is becoming more and more severe the time comes to end the situation. Reach out to an individual from your family or a close an acquaintance for help. If the person continues to commit violence , only to return with a plea for forgiveness, and promises you that he'll change the way he behaves, you should be aware of the deceit that is going on. Do you have something giving him that he isn't willing to be loved if you decide to decide to leave? Maybe you're supporting the man financially, or any other way. This support must be ended immediately. If this occurs the manipulator is likely to go on to locate someone that can help the manipulator in the same manner. They may seek out another person in his circle that is susceptible to manipulation and abuse. Make sure you warn your friends and everyone else susceptible to his ulterior motives, and then move yourself as far from him as you can.

It's a very difficult thing to go through and sometimes, you need to come to an age that certain people aren't going to change or "get better," the way you would like to see them. Parents of children who abuse drugs face the most difficult moment when their children arrive home, pleading for their parents as children, then soliciting money from parents know that they'll use on drugs. What should a parent do in this case? There's no simple solution since emotional attachment is among the most powerful experiences humans can go through. Sometimes we have to decide that the pain we endure is worth the abuser who is on our side. There are others who reach a moment at which they are forced to decide to leave, having endured enough of being bullied and being abused. Be aware of the warning signs an early point is the best way to stop the situation from becoming one that sees everyone becoming hurt repeatedly time as part of the vicious cycle of attachment, love and abuse as well as false reconciliation.

Chapter 7: What Is Dark Nlp?

Although some individuals may choose to employ these dark psychology techniques to harm their victims There are instances that you can employ these strategies with no intention of manipulating someone else. These tactics were intentionally or unintentionally added to our toolbox by different sources. These might include:

* As as a young person, you'd observe how adults, particularly the ones you were close to were treated.

* As an teen, your mind and the ability to fully comprehend the actions that you encountered were heightened.

* You were able observe other people using the techniques and eventually succeed.

The strategies might have started out as unintentional at first however, once you realized that they worked to get you the results you desired and you began to employ those strategies in a deliberate manner.

Some individuals, such as politicians, public speaker or salesperson, will be taught to use these strategies to achieve what they want.

Dark Psychology Tactics That Are Commonly Used

"Love flooding" could include praise, buttering up or congratulating someone to make them accept the suggestion you'd like to get. If you need someone to assist you in moving things into your home It is possible to employ the power of love to get them feeling happy and increase the likelihood to help them. Dark manipulators may also employ it to make another person feel a sense of belonging to them, and force them to do actions they might not usually do.

"Liars": It can involve giving the victim a false version of what happened. This could also mean an exaggeration or a part of the truth to achieve what you want to achieve.

"Love denial": This is difficult for the victim as it could cause them to feel disenchanted and unloved to the con artist. This can mean

denying affection and love until you get what you want from the victim.
"Withdrawal." This could be when the person being treated receives silent treatment or is not allowed to be treated until they can meet the requirements of the other person.

* Limiting choices: The manipulator could allow their victim to certain options However, they do this in order to divert attention away from making choices they do not want their victim to make.

* Semantic manipulation It is a method that involves manipulators using certain words that are commonly used which are accepted significance by both parties in a dialogue. Then, they inform the victim later that they meant something entirely different when they spoke the word. This new definition is usually will alter the definition completely and result in the conversation proceeds as the manipulator would like regardless of whether the victim was manipulated.
Reverse psychology is when you ask

someone to perform something in a certain way, but knowing that they'll perform the opposite. The opposite is the one you wanted to occur initially.

Who is likely to make use of dark Techniques?

A variety of people could choose to employ these strategies against you. They are found all over your life and that's why it's so crucial to be aware of how to stay clear of these tactics. The people who use these techniques of dark psychology deliberately are:

* Narcissists: They will be able to create an exaggerated belief in their self-worth and have to convince others believe they are more superior than others. To fulfill their desire of being loved and worshipped by all who meet them; they'll use persuasion as well as dark psychological techniques.

* Sociopaths: People that are social psychopathic are charming, smart and convincing. However, they act in such a way in order to obtain what they desire. They

don't have any feelings and aren't in a position to feel any guilt. That means they'll are not afraid to use methods of dark psychology to obtain what they want. This includes getting to create superficial relationships.

* Political leaders: With the aid of dark psychological techniques, a politician can persuade someone to cast votes for them through convincing people that the viewpoint is the best one.

* Salespeople Do not all salespeople are likely to resort to using tricks to get you. However, it's probable that some people, particularly those who are genuinely interested in the numbers they are able to generate and are the most effective they can be, won't think twice about using dark methods to influence others.

* Leaders: Over the course of the history of mankind there have been plenty of leaders who have employed the tactics of dark psychology to convince their subordinates, team members and even their citizens to

perform the actions they wish.

* Selfish people: This could include anyone who makes sure their personal needs are placed ahead of everyone else's. They aren't worried about other people and are willing to let others sacrifice their rights to gain. If it benefits them then it's fine if it helps someone else. If someone is the losing party, it's the person who loses, not them.

This list is essential as it can serve two purposes. The first is to aid you in becoming more aware of people who might try to influence you into doing something you aren't willing to do. Secondly, it could help you in self-realization. Be on the lookout for people who are trying to take something away from you, with no worries regarding how it might affect your life, is one of the major purposes of this guidebook to ensure that you can protect yourself against the dark side of psychology.

Understanding the Art of Manipulation

What, then is it that we encounter in our daily life, do we have to be vigilant about?

Persuasive Language

The saying that every image tells a story is extremely accurate. Words can be more powerful when they motivate and inspire us, sometimes to the level of manipulating. Have you ever been encouraged by a great speaker, whom's daring words spur you to actions? Words can influence us even when we're lost in a book. The art of language can be persuasive in influencing us to believe in something, even when the eyes are telling us different. Communication is an effective instrument, particularly in convincing people to take action.

Salespeople and marketers make use of language to convince us that their customers that their products are what we're looking for. Making use of words, such as:

The price is affordable; it's easy to use; secure and enjoyable. Time-saving sure to last.

Take note of how these phrases give us the impression that they're confident about their products.

* Politicians may use words like:

O "We" to include you within their universe. "We" and "Us" to let you feel part of a group.

* Bullies employ language, as well as aggressive behavior to accomplish their own selfish goals.

Criminal predators, like sociopaths and psychopaths as well as Narcissists, are all those who are able to use persuasive language. This is a method to gain control and control the other person.

All of these are communication strategies to let us feel accepted which is why they are important.

CHAPTER 8: THE TYPES OF HUMAN BEHAVIOR

The reason a large number of people fail to understand the human behavior is because they observe their behavior without considering the various aspects.

Similar to how people behave and you won't be able to understand the human behavior until you consider the person's beliefs as well as values, ways of life, perception and each other aspect that impacts his behavior in a straightforward or circular manner.

The person we are is the result from a myriad of influences. Conditions, qualities and, of course our childhood. We can effectively process and interact with a constantly evolving world. While we explore the world around us, we adapt and get better at certain methods to survive. What can we do to clarify why we do what we do? The good news is that science can help us understand the behavior of humans.

Experiments in Science That Help Us Understand Human Behavior

The Reason We Give Credit to ourselves, yet blame others when we have Failed?

To fully comprehend the world, all events should have some significance or reason that is behind their significance or purpose. This helps us understand what's going on. We'll generally be able to recognize this reasoning in regards to our behavior.

This is the theory of attribution.

There are two types of attributing:

* Internal attribution -- where we assign the causes to internal factors (ourselves)
* External attribution - where we attribute causes to external factors (others)

If we've achieved our goal in our endeavor, we must use inward attribution, acknowledging that we're accountable for our success. On the other hand, in the chance that we fall short or make a mistake, we'll need to use external attributing. This wasn't the fault of us that was beyond our capability to fix were the fault of others. And what's the motive that we're doing this? The main reason is to be seen in a decent light. We'd rather not admit that we have been disappointed due to our mistakes. Another possibility is that, by using the attributions we are protecting ourselves. If we are able to accuse someone else and avoid punishment or criticisms.

In any event, a closer look will show that we aren't helping ourselves with these self-serving attributions. A specific study showed that people with greater experience generally, have less self-serving claims. This helped them focus more on the actual reasons that kept them back. In this way they could improve their appearance.

This is one of the theories that studying human behavior could help us to make improvements.

Why do we subsequently accept what We Hear, See, and read?

We are blessed with freedom, isn't it? Furthermore, we are certainly the most intelligent creatures on the planet. Therefore, before we evaluate a situation we weigh up each of the benefits and negatives. We consider everything we see. Very. Actually, the opposite is also true. Instead, we are naturally disposed to take whatever is put in front of us. In addition, you are aware of the is a well-known axiom--"truth is more interesting than fiction?" In fact, it is applicable to what we read and hear.

This is the automatic way of thinking. That's it. why do we naturally believe the news we receive? An continuing investigation (2018) that examines the reasons why people fall prey to fake information, and believe that it is because we're tired. The investigation looked into the motives for trusting "conspicuously incorrect articles" and found that the inability to fake news is fueled by the slowness of our pace. It may seem quite brutal, but there's something to it. Previous research suggests that fatigue is the main issue. In one experiment, members were invited to propose imprisonment in the aftermath of reading about wrongdoing. This gave the accounts of two of the guilty parties. The members were informed that in the report on wrongdoing, any false declarations were marked in red.

In the meantime, a lot of the participants were distracted as the other members completed the test under normal conditions. In the event that the test participants were diverted, they did not get the chance to think about the fake articulations, and instead handed long sentences of the burglar.

However I think it's much far more. It is essential to make in the moment with our judgments in our daily lives. Additionally, because of this, our senses come into action and we rely on previous experiences. Since we have to react swiftly, it's a good idea to be able to recognize the things we observe and hear.

Our forefathers weren't able to relax and contemplate whether it was a huge mammoth who was tromping over them. Whatever the case the circumstances differ. This idea can assist in understanding human behavior specifically under certain situations. For instance our judgment may be impaired when we're tired and distracted.

Why do we prefer to be Different and Comparative Different Kinds of People?

We all are averse to our friends and relatives, as well as associates even our accomplices. What ever it is which of them have in common in all respects? They're likely to be essentially similar to us.

This is Social Comparison Theory.

We discover about ourselves and our capabilities by comparing ourselves to other people. We want to think about our lives. However that we cannot do this without any correlation. That's why the reason why we simply compare people who have a similarity to us?

Secrets of the Mind Secrets of the Mind
We are a part of a small universe with a few and common possible results. Our cerebrums guide and contrast us with the most plausible version of what we're used to regardless of whether this is a result of vocation-based decisions or extraordinary romantic love and does not contrast our ideals with the best of what's. This is due to the fact that, more than any other lengthy periods of development the cerebrums of our brains have evolved to follow certain designed traits like security, abundance (riches) as well as forward motion and tranquility. These designed needs protected our minds from deceitful situations as well as insecurity, enemies, and deceit. They allowed us to maintain the distance of a situation which were active, situations that could challenge our minds as far as they could. This book will explore the various methods and courses that can be used to unlock the maximum potential that everyone is pondering.

The first step is to unwire Your Brain

As the science says it is difficult for people to be in the same constant condition. It is because we're either getting knack of it, blurring it and developing or falling. We can see this in the life of our cells and the passing of time. They decide whether to grow or to eat dust. Similar things happen in our brains, and neurons, the cells responsible for transmitting information all throughout our bodies, will also decide to grow or disappear. This leads to a process known as live wiring, in which neurons create and remodel the components in your system of sensory over time. How can you harness this power and encourage your cells to select up on the development? Through doing the following:

1. Make a conscious effort to be constantly inquisitive: You should take the initiative to be curious about the general environment, your circumstances and the immediate environment. Instead of waking at the morning ready for your daily practice and a

planned day, try to become more attentive and conscious of the world your faculties are exposed to. As you are open to a boost and usually ask questions regarding it, you're putting your brain to move into an animated domain. The mind is compelled to further dissect and create new ideas and analyze the issues it perceives. In the event that you find this difficult at the beginning, try to imagine your self as an uninvolved observer at the world in a particular context.

2. Take a moment before responding Your primary thought that you have in mind when you respond doesn't necessarily reflect the reality of who you are. This is our natural tendencies that our minds then jump to due to the perception of examples. When you stop reacting to a situation or misfortune you have the opportunity to decide on your most enthusiastic reaction. This lets you take responsibility for the event or perhaps your response to it. A method to practice this short, instant

reaction model is through the use of perception scenarios. Imagine you're grinding on your computer, and your manager is sending you an email concerning this or that and imagine how you'd like to react instead of giving in to your first instinctual reaction.

3. Decide to have a positive and tangible difference in the world. Remember that it's not about what other people think of you. Therefore, if you find yourself playing to the tune of internet visits, preferences and hearts, realize that it's not always fulfilling your needs. Instead, try to constantly be directing yourself toward the things that provide you with worth and wisdom. This will enable you to constantly be thinking , and thus constantly rewiring your brain.

The Second Way: Concentrate on Your Health

In addition to pushing our neurons to grow in a variety of ways, we can also force our bodies to produce new nerve cells by an process known as neurogenesis. What is an advantage for us to discover the mind's mysteries? It could improve your memory, provide mental security of your mind, and even reverse the harm of the use of drugs. Neurogenesis can open the possibility to enhance our psychological well-being as well as increasing our capacity to think. Learn to do the things that follow.

1. You must ensure that you are getting adequate sleep. If you're not getting enough sleep and you are not getting enough sleep your body won't be able to repair itself, or build new, re-structured, or new neurons. You should be taking an adequate amount of rest and is in line with a regular schedule.

2. Reduce stress levels: An anxious life prevents your brain from having the ability to create new cells. the delay in pressure can cause many physical ailments and mental fatigue. Make sure you have a morning and a daily routine that you stick to, then focus into consideration what you are able to achieve on a regular basis and make some time to be outdoors and

exercise.

3. Read extensively (and study) books: They are like tiny enchantments for the brain. They help you open more effective ways to use the brain, build a bigger network of thoughts and increase your understanding about intellectual skills, intellectual abilities, and the language. The more you read and study the better your brain will function and expand.

4. Get rid of harmful substances: Alcohol and drugs can alter an arrangement that is created by new memories and hinder the development of new connections, and impede the development of new neurons.

5. Intermittent fast (cut calories) If you are able to perform a continuous fasting or restricting calories it is possible to lower the level of leptin in your blood and force your body to autophagy, which is the stage where your cell phones flush rid of poisons and eliminate waste.

Chapter 9: The Psychological Basis Of Dreams

The psychoanalytic interpretation of dreaming or psycho-physiological mechanism of dreaming is used in the study of psychology behind dreams. So, there are two school of thought regarding the field of psychology of dreams: The first believes in the relation to REM asleep and the dream, and the importance of dreams in the process of learning and that dreaming occurs as the result of random neural firings which result in random images that could or might not have a significance; the other is that dreams happen due to unrepressed and unconscious impulses that could be explained by psychoanalytic symbols and could help explain psychic phenomena or help in understanding the root causes of mental illness.

"Dreams are the path to the unconscious according to Freud as they can be examined in a manner that can reveal the subconscious's hidden desires. Thus dreams reveal the person we are and what we desire and the way we plan to accomplish these goals. However, a number of modern psychologists have discarded the interpretation of dreams as semantic by focusing on repressed impulses and the meaning behind them.' They believe that dreams arise from spontaneous neural firings within the brain when the body rests and creating pictures in the brain.

There are various stages during sleep There are several stages of sleep, and REM asleep is the most advanced stage. Dreams are connected to the REM (rapid eye movements) stage of sleep and we are more likely to experience many dreams in one night, but we do are able to forget the majority of these dreams. We do not play out these dreams as, when we dream the body is subjected to temporary paralysis, which is a defense and bodily defence mechanism to protect against any external harm.

According to psychologists, dreaming is also a defence method since all unrepressed desires that could cause harm on our minds are released by dreams. Thus, both physically and psychologically dreams perform defensive or protective roles in releasing traumatizing thoughts, stress and impulses that are suppressed. They also protecting the body from injury external to it. Recollection of dreams and control over them by means of lucid dreaming and hypnosis which are more commonly used by psychotherapists who are traditional aren't very common nowadays. But, these techniques provide deeper insights into the imagery of dreams and the ways in which they can be stimulated or provoked in psychotherapeutic sessions. They can also be retained and then interpreted to give greater insight into the subconscious.

The physiological basis of the REM phase of sleep could explain the reason why we can dream of specific images. But, this mechanism may be ineffective in determining the reason why certain images appear. Certain theories suggest that certain thoughts, desire or events may manifest in dreams as images. Trauma or any other incident that has significant emotional significance could trigger repeated dreams that contain the same images. Based on the literature available I suggest that dreams may have five primary functions: the clinical purpose of explaining mental disease, a cognitive purpose that aids in learning and an adaptive purpose in restoring body systems and a cathartic purpose of releasing painful or suppressed emotions, and a defensive purpose of providing a protection for the mind as well as the body. Therefore, dreams can be explained from both psycho-physiological and psychoanalytic perspectives. It is essential to understand psychoanalysis as well as psychophysiology as well as incorporate dreams from both areas to understand the full range of the mental processes involved.

The five main functions of dreams are listed in this article, and the fundamental theory of a complete dream theory must be based on these five aspects.

Functional Clinical Effects of Dreams Certain psychologists believe that dreams are connected to mental disease. A lot of post-traumatic dreams are associated with anxiety. Furthermore, prolonged or frequent traumatic nightmares may be the first sign of mental illness or failure in biological functions within the body. The majority of mental illnesses can be traced back to specific dreams. Understanding the reasons why dreams happen to specific individuals may help to understand the causes of mental illnesses. The clinical significance of dreams has been acknowledged in psychoanalysis, however its full potential is not fully understood in the field of physiology. Additional research on the subject is required to determine the significance of dreams in describing and preventing or the treatment of physical or mental ailments. The dreaming process could reveal the brain's disorders, brain diseases as well as hormonal changes in the body. They could also have the clinical benefit of identifying various ailments and abnormalities within the body.

Cognitive function of Dreams The Cognitive Function of Dreams Dreams can be beneficial in the process of learning. Studies have shown that dreams play an important crucial cognitive role in children , who have numerous dreams and more REM sleeping time than adult. consequently, children learn while they are dreaming and REM sleep may be beneficial on the development of physical skills. It is possible that dreams may also offer insight into the problems and solutions, and a myriad of discoveries in the form of inventions, discoveries, and new ideas come to light. Dreams can reveal many possibilities for our thinking process and, by combining them, they offer solutions for cognitive problems to some of our personal objectives. So, they can be highly effective tools for learning assist in self-understanding, realization, and help improve and strengthen cognitive capabilities.

Dreams that are adaptive - The ability to dream helps us adapt to the environment around us. While the evolutionary benefit of dreams isn't clear or not studied in depth, the fact we are able to continue to dream and even learn about and defend ourselves in dreams makes dreams an essential element of our active lives. The adaptive purpose of dreams is beneficial for the body since it assists in restoring the mental, bodily and physical equilibrium. Though this is still a controversial view, the complete physical and psychological benefits must be examined from an evolutionary standpoint.

The cathartic function of dreams The cathartic function of dreams is that they are extremely therapeutic. Through the symbolism of images, they ease stress and eliminate our anxieties, urges and desires, as well as help us to confront our mental state. Dreams are not just the traditional route to the subconscious' and are fundamental shields to help us defend ourselves and get rid of our stress. The emotions and thoughts which are frightening, painful, humiliating or even dangerous to face in real life are reflected in dreams, and they help us face the realities of life. Psychoanalytically, dreams symbolize the fulfillment of wishes, and numerous images from dreams, such as extended objects are believed to be as a symbol for sexual organs. It is not clear whether every dream is an expression of wish fulfillment or not, some dreams may be a source of anxiety, or even contrary to any desire fulfillment. If you find yourself dreaming about your injury or that of your family members. If so you're dissolving your anxiety in dreams that could assist you in functioning better and more secure in the real world.

Dreams' defensive function The reason for this is the cathartic and adaptive function of dreams in releasing through catharsis. We also adjust to the environment. This allows the body with a shield or defense that allows the body and mind to function without injury or obstruction. Although this notion isn't popular with psychologists, it is believed that dreams can have significant protective roles. In addition, when we experience physiological changes within our bodies including that of the release of Glycine an amino acid, which is the defense mechanism. Mental and physical irritations can be relieved through dreams creating a barrier for the mind and body. So, dreams are not only the royal road to the unconscious' but are vital shields or covers to shield the mind or body from excessive stress. As your boiling kettle comes with features to let out excessive steam, dreams act as a regulating mechanism to eliminate any excesses in the body and mind. Dreams are the mind's excretions. Numerous scientists have supported the notion that dreams are of no evolutionary benefit and no value. But, if you look more deeply into the history of psychological research, the importance of dreams in describing mental life cannot be denied. Further research into the field of physiology, imaging techniques and psychotherapy that explore the psychology behind dreams could reveal the reason we have dreams and whether they are simply a way of regulating or not.

CHAPTER 10: THE 10 MOST EFFECTIVE TECHNIQUES OF DARK PSYCHOLOGY

1. Love Bombing

Love bombing is a method that many manipulators of emotions employ when dealing to their victim. It involves a ferocious rapid, impulsive, and powerful display of positive feelings towards victims. This might seem odd at first when discussing CEM. If the person manipulating is trying to hurt anyone then why would they want to boost the happiness towards the person in front of them? This is because it could help them achieve their goals.

The reason for using love bombing is to generate a strong sense of love, trust and compliant by the victim towards their manipulator. The degree that love bombing can be utilized, as well as the person who it is used on, will largely depend on the perception of the manipulator the situation.

Someone who is isolated, in need of support as well as comfort will be more likely targeted by love bombs and more intensely than other people. If the victim appears more grounded, they may require a more restrained and perhaps more subtle method of loving bombing.

2. Active-Aggressive Revenge

Active-aggressive revenge is similar in concept to cold treatment, in the sense that the manipulator largely ignores the victim as a method of punishment. There is only one difference: manipulators behave with a stubborn attitude rather than cut off communication completely. They make up fake smiles in order to show that they do not feel hurt However, their actions, like the way they speak, convey an entirely different story. If the victim attempts to confront the manipulator, he will come up with a fake reason to leave.

In the same way, if the victim is trying to communicate with their manipulator, they could be rude. They'll pretend to forget about things in order to get rid of the victim. Even worse, instead of openly discuss concerns with the person who is affected they will resort to retaliation.

3. The ambiguous reality

Individuals who fall into the hands of skilled manipulators will find their opinions turned into absurdity. In simple terms, if you do not agree with a harmful person, they'll frame your words to make it appear absurd and sexist. If, for instance, you ask them to stop talking about you in a rude way and they respond with statements like "So you think that you're superior to me, but not me, right?" This technique is often referred to as misrepresenting or confusing the reality. The goal is to evoke guilt, and all they do is share their emotions.

If they are manipulators They believe that they are able to read other's minds and see their motives. This is the reason they jump to conclusions based upon fact instead of reality. It is possible to describe this method as the practice of putting words into people's mouths and blame them for their actions. Psychologists say that manipulators are aware of their dark side and swiftly accuse others of portraying them as evil. In essence, the trick of conflating reality is for them a type of self-defense.

4. Reality Denial

One of the most terrifying things that humans might experience is the sensation that they're losing their sense of sanity. This can be a nightmare in the event that it's explained by something the victim is able to comprehend, for instance, the result of stress. However, this could be a bit disturbing in the event that the emotional manipulator causes this sanity-like feeling. Reality denial is various techniques employed in CEM that are aimed at to destroy the sanity of the victim in order to pursue selfish motives. The manner in which this happens, as well as its effects, will vary according to the method that is most effective for the victim.

One of the principal tenets of denial of

reality is that it takes place gradually. If the manipulator attempts to accomplish all of this in one go the victim will see and remain away. Due to this, the person manipulating will probably not immediately set out to ruin the victim's sanity in a matter of minutes. This type of scenario is nearly impossible to accomplish without being caught.

5. Projection

Projection is the process of not being able to recognize your own shortcomings, and then using every possible method to blame yourself for these. The process displaces one's negative behaviour and assigns the blame to another. Although everyone engages to project from time time, manipulators use excessively, and adds to be emotionally violent. Instead of accepting their mistakes as flaws, flaws, or imperfections an manipulator will dump the blame on others in a cruel and in pain. This means that the manipulator is unable to stop the behavior and seek improvements or corrections The victims are embarrassed and feel responsible for what they did not take responsibility for.

6. Indirect Insults

Name-calling and insults are both direct types of aggression and abuse. An insecure person is aware of this and will resort to tactics to ensure that they are not accused of insulting or calling their subjects names. They will then be able to think of the attack as raw and then find a way to disguise it using different words so it looks less vicious. The insults could be discreetly used, like sarcasm or a calm tone, to mislead the audience. The victim may believe they're being offered suggestions, given solutions, assisted or even taught something, however, they are actually being insulted. But the manipulator is aware that their motives aren't authentic, but are designed to discredit the victim's skills and self-confidence. These veiled insults are often referred to as insults that are not directly addressed. While the insults are sugar-coated those who suffer from them know that they've been sabotaged. This can cause suffering and pain, particularly because the person who is manipulating them could be someone close like an alleged lover, sibling or friend, boss, teacher, or coworker.

7. Triangulation

Triangulation is a different powerful weapon that can be used to influence individuals. The manipulator is an outside party in their relationship with another. They want to inform their victim that a third party could be employed to be replaced at any time. As soon as the fear sets in the victim is then forced to follow the wishes of the manipulator in they fear losing their identity or being replaced. The other party may not be explicitly portrayed as being the same as the victim However, the manipulator will ensure that the victim knows about someone else who the person in the lie likes. If the victim inquires about the person who is not theirs they are portrayed as being jealous, insecure or insensitive. The manipulator will keep the situation under control when they get to this point. However the issue is trying to make more effort in order to delight the manipulator in order to keep them in the loop.

8. Silent Treatment

It is referred to as stonewalling or withholding. It's the process where an individual, after feeling that they have been wronged by you is cut off from communication, and uses either physical or emotional withdrawal in order to express their anger. This is what we mostly faced as kids. As children, if we were not allowed something or our parents were harsh with our behavior, then we'd complain and beg them to stop until they redeemed it for us. I'm sure that you think of this. We were once tiny manipulators!

We could have had manipulators in our lives, but the outcome wasn't harmful. A cold treatment can be harmful when it is used to communicate the impression of disdain and shaming. The manipulator transmits the message that an individual isn't worthy of their attention or attention, love and the list goes on. The implicit message is it is that the target is unimportant and cannot exist without them. If they do succeed the victim is embarrassed and helpless. Psychologists describe cold treatment as torture since humans require recognition of their existence, and especially by those close to them. Although cold treatment can be described as not a way to communicate however, it is in reality, a clear signal which you can either use the game of the manipulator or be a victim.

9. Blackmailing

Blackmailing is yet another popular technique used to manipulate the process. This involves making use of threats that are not justified to gain an advantage or get one's demands met. It is also considered to be coercion. The manipulator employs this technique to make subjects follow their own wishes or to purchase something they desire. The manipulator will take time to research the victim in order to be successful. They are able to identify personal traits and secrets that can be harmful to the person who is discovered. For instance, a man could threaten to expose the truth regarding a woman who does not have sexual contact with them. Some manipulators be so bold as to threaten physical harm to their subjects or their family members when they don't adhere to their demands.

10. Shame

Shame is an effective method employed by manipulators to harm the self-esteem and determination of the victims. The manipulator looks at the people who they are proud of, and then targets the subjects they are proud of and targets them. Through shaming and/or making the victim feel that they've made a mistake and are ashamed of themselves, any confidence and self-esteem the victim might have lost. The toxic people love to learn about their victims' wounds and scars as they can provide a formidable arsenal for in the future. They can be so brutal that they could use injuries like the trauma of childhood abuse to afflict their victims.

CHAPTER 11: SEDUCTION USING DARK PSYCHOLOGY

Seduction is the act of entice others into a relationship , or sexual behaviour. It could be described as the practice of convincing those who may not initially want to be convinced initially and is usually by virtue of sexual or physical attraction. It is a technique which can prove helpful if you're trying to establish yourself in long-term relationships or are looking to reignite the passion you share with your partner. In the end, the way to express love is universal. Everybody would like feeling loved and valued.

Define Seduction
Seduction is basically the act of taking another person's attention away. In fact the etymological meaning of the word"seduce" comes in the Latin word which means "leading to a wrong direction" and "to

alter." In that mind, you could conclude that the primary nature of seduction is negative. It's about convincing the other person into doing something that might not have considered acceptable in different situations. But, it's something which has endured over many thousands of years of human history and it will not be going away. It is crucial to remember one specific aspect--there is a distinction between seduction and rape. Seduction is the forceful sexual contact with a person against their will while seduction involves seeking out another person, perhaps against their wishes until they give agree to it. It is vital to keep in mind that when you attempt to seduce someone else it is important to respect consent , or absence of it.
Selecting the Target

The first step to seduce someone else is to identify the goal. In the brief discussion in the article, the most important factor to consider is that the person you are trying to seduce must be open to the notion of being enticed. If it doesn't appear as if will ever be a victim of your methods, or if they do not respond to your attempts pushing them forward and trying to convince them could be a step too far between coercion and seduction. Remember, when you seduce you are trying to pursue the person you want to seduce until the target is instead chasing you. This means you are able to pursue another person however you're only doing so to get them to pursue you. If they don't follow you, you'll not be able to lure them, and they are ready to go to another person.

In addition to being open to your charms and efforts to charm, the most effective people to target are those which you are able to sense that they're not they can fill. They might be feeling lonely or self-conscious and would like to be noticed. You can capitalize on this desire and apply it for your own advantage by pursuing the person you want to pursue knowing that you're satisfying a part of them that they didn't think to fill. They are usually lonely and unsatisfied, or are able to be transformed into an unhappy, isolated person with little effort on your part. Keep in mind that one who is happy with life isn't likely to be attracted by being enticed. It is important to ensure that the person you'd like to impress is not happy, but that they appeal to you, too. If they don't bring out intense emotions in you then you're not likely to be able to maintain an interest in the subject. You won't take pleasure in the chase or excitement if you think the target isn't quite the right one for you.

Techniques for Seducing
After you've chosen the person you want to target and confirmed that the person you want to talk to will be open to you then you are now ready to start the art of seduction. There are a variety of methods you can employ to charm an individual. It's just the

matter of choosing the one that is most suitable for you, and which one you believe you'd like to try. Check out this list and start to think about which one is best for you and the person you are trying to impress. Keep in mind that there are no two targets that are alike as a result there's no universal strategy for how to charm the person you want to attract. You are ultimately doing the same thing: find the person to target to cause them to feel vulnerable and get them feel awed by your company and reap the benefits. The method you follow to complete these steps will differ between individuals.

Incite the other person to be nervous.
As was briefly mentioned the people who are satisfied with the way things have been for them is not likely to desire to be lured by someone else. Actually, they'll not even be interested since they don't think they're

being left out of any particular thing. Sometimes you may bypass this step by seeking out those who are showing signs of anger and frustration however, at in other instances, you will need to make an effort to make your partner feel nervous.

Of course, you're likely to want to do this as secretly as you can. You would prefer not to have someone else to know the details of what you're doing and they're not likely to be interested in you. In the end, few people would want to be around those who they suspect are trying to undermine their own goals. Consider rereading the sections on hidden manipulating, influence on emotions and mind control, if you are not sure what strategies you could use to gradually, but effectively, destroy self-esteem and create a more controlled victim.

Be flexible to other people's preferences
If you're looking to attract someone but aren't keen on a relationship that lasts for

long The most efficient way to achieve this is by creating a false sense of self. It is best to focus into consideration the characteristics your prospective partner likes, solely because you want to lure the person you are trying to impress. It is not necessary to develop a permanent passion for weaving underwater However, you should pretend to be interested it if it's something your target is interested in as well.

Sweet talking
Many people are ineffective listeners, especially in the case of not getting what they would like to hear. If you are aware of this and begin to recognize this fact, you can start to draw the attention of other people simply by letting them know what you desire to hear. If they're hearing what they want to hear from you, they're likely to pay attention. After all, why would they not when you are giving them whatever they are looking for at the moment? To seduce

them you, you need to be able to master knowing the things they want to convey and then delivering the right phrases. It will increase their confidence and make them feel happier and make them addicted with the messages you tell them into their ears. Eventually, they will be more interested in following.

It's a matter of Temptation
There's a reason that it is that temptation appears in a myriad of stories and myths - it's extremely persuading. If you try to lure someone by offering them a tiny hint of what might get if they partnered with you, you're essentially playing a game with the other person. The person you are teasing could become obsessed with that small glimpse, and then start trying to find it. It is basically creating a desire in someone else which they are unable to resist or deny. If you are able to find the something that ignites this desire, they'll be inclined to follow your lead when you provide the

chance to accomplish the goal they are looking for initially.

You can be the parent of your target
In the end, people tend to be more connected to their fondest memories. For most of us, the most memorable events were in childhood and involved parents in some way. You can relive the feelings of childhood if you're capable of putting yourself into the role of a parent without being obvious. Try to provide some kind of support to the person you are caring for, describing that you are interested in their wellbeing and wishing to assist however you can and you'll be able to bring them back to the feeling of secure attachment which, in turn, will make them more likely to want to be around you.

Insinuations
Insinuating things, which is being able to instil an idea in someone's mind by using subtle, indirect language is particularly

useful in attempting to entice someone else. By doing this you create doubt, and when there is uncertain times, you effectively influence the person into doing what you want them to. You could say that you're interested in someone else without speaking, which could cause the person to be more interested in being interested in you initially.

Suspense
If you are in suspense, your audience will be in awe of you. They're not certain of what to anticipate, which makes you fascinating. They will want to follow your story to see what's going to happen next, because you're so unpredictable. If you're looking to keep the suspense, it is essential to constantly come up with ways to keep the tension running. Always try to come up with ideas that seem unexpected, simply because it helps keep people (and your potential target) attracted to your character. They'll be attracted by your spontaneity and

interest in following you , while you are in complete the control of where your relationship is headed.

CHAPTER 12: RECOGNIZING THE LIAR

If you turn into manipulator, it's just your lies that needs to be true. Everyone else shouldn't be able to tell the truth other than you. So , how do you identify the fake liars and ensure that you're the only person left? Do you think it is possible to detect a lie without strapping them to the lie detector? The answer is a resounding yes. Psychologically speaking, it's simpler to speak the truth rather than lie, but humans tend to choose the latter. If you lie you're using an excessive amount of energy and muscles. All of these lying energies and muscles are revealed by the body language of the person and hidden emotions. If you are able to identify these hidden body language and feelings, you'll be able to discern virtually anyone. First, you must learn to recognize and decode human deceit. Human being could encounter 200 lies within a single day. Imagine, 200 lies directed at you. However If you are able to fabricate a lie that is not the truth, these numbers won't be applicable to you.

To stop being victimized by lies, first you need to acquire some understanding of how people can be successful in lying. You also need to take some time to learn how to be an effective lie-detector. It's not something that happens in a flash.

In determining lying gender plays a significant factor. It's the truth that women are more lying than males. They are not just adept in lying, but they are also adept in detecting falsehoods of their peers. Men aren't aware of how to deceive a lie. For them, a perfect lie is just something like "I'm not hungry. Women are, however can be able to come up with a more sophisticated and credible lies.

Although women do are more adept at telling lies and detecting them but a significant portion of lies go unnoticed regardless of gender. It's difficult to discern the truth from the fiction because when someone is convinced that the lie they're describing is true the audience will be forced to believe in them as well. Natural born lie detectors boast astonishingly high accuracy of 80% in identifying lies. They are also known as truth-seekers. They don't require prior experience to determine the difference between lying and truth. If you're interested in knowing how rare they are be aware of this number. From a pool of 20,000 individuals only 50 can be considered truth wizards. But, we're not in this article to boast about the existence of truth-seekers but to make an effort to become an one. We must first dispel some of the false myths.

Debuting Popular Lying Myths
If you think that spotting the lie is simple to spot, then you're in beyond your capabilities. There isn't a secret formula to spot the lie. One cannot be deemed lying by the fact that they are prone to sweating and

fidget or have odd eye motions. To learn a thing of a thing or two regarding liars we must put aside everything we've seen in Hollywood films and TV shows.

1. If you glance at the left side while speaking you're lying

This method isn't efficient in distinguishing lies from truth. Psychology and science have several points to make regarding the movement of the eyes of humans, however it doesn't mean that we should take everything as gospel. There are a variety of reasons for someone to turn their eyes away when conversing with you. One reason could be the possibility that they are uneasy with your presence or it could be a habit that they learned as a child.

False Myth #2 If you are unable to look at your eyes, you're a fraud

We are all naturally shy. An extended eye contact can instantly make us look away. It is absolutely nothing to do with deceitful features. However anyone who wants to deceive you will not be able to look away.

They'll want to ensure that you are convinced of every lies they're telling you. In order to achieve their goal, they'll stare you straight in the eyes while they lie.

The Myth of the 3rd Child 3: Children are professional lying liars

Many people prefer to think of lying as a child. Although children are innocent but their patterns of lying can't be as convincing as the deceitful tracks that adults employ to spread their lies. A child can be lying to you and not conceal the evidence behind their deceit. An adult who lies would not be so reckless. Children who are younger than eight years old cannot be labeled as honest liars, unless you truly would like them to be able to be able to get away with it. It's that when children reach the age range that they begin to look for ways to be more manipulative in their lies. A child might be lying about not eating cake, while putting an edible cake layer over their faces. How do they qualify as professional lying people? It is only possible to be an expert liar if are able to get away with the lies.

Myth #4: Texts and emails, and other online technologies are a reservoir for lies

There is no doubt that emails and texts can contain truth, but it's not the case that texts or emails make it simple to tell a lie. It's not about hiding a lie using technology. an untruth, but rather the goal of the lie. Consider it this way: the primary reason individuals would make use of these platforms to aid in the spread of an act of deceit is when they're looking for details held by someone who is who is on their list of targets.

An example of a real-life scenario that dispels this myth is those who are in the pool of dating. The majority of them are enticed to lie about their profile to find the perfect partner. These sites aren't packed with those with lying tendencies and a few with the intention of lying. For them, lying isn't an attribute, but rather an attribute that is meant to gain them something. The online fraudsters are also taking this method. They begin by looking for someone with an item of information that could be useful to them. Then, they look for ways to persuade the individual to give them the information.

We've covered the initial step needed to identify a lie. It's identifying the purpose of the lies. If the lie causes you to lose a valuable item of information, especially on a platform that is technological that is not a platform, it loses the status of a deceit and turns into an illegal activity. It is no longer a case of dealing with a lying liar and a criminal suspect.

Debunking the Pathological Liar

If someone once called you an egregious liar, they really believed that you were expert in the art of writing lies. They believe you're an unflinching serial liar that has no regrets for the consequences that result from the lies. According to scientific research the more committed lying liar is the victim of psychopathy, which is a personality disorder. Psychopathy sufferers are self-centered, lacking empathy, social skills, and are often unable to form meaningful connections with people around them.

To be a pathological lie-teller, feeling guilt is not a feature on a resume. People who are pathological liars often feel genuinely sorry for people who tend to take things too seriously. In the end the first step to being a credible liar is not to feel any guilt. The emotion of guilt can be seen in your face. The majority of liars are found guilty because they display guilt on their faces while trying to deceive. If you are able to keep away the guilt associated with lying it's as simple as breathing into and out.

A good lying liar will always be quick in their words, so don't count on someone's hesitation to be an indicator that a lie is crafted. Perhaps this person is someone who has a stammer or perhaps has some unidentified difficulties with speech when being they are being interrogated or in a stressful situation. The maze of the human brain can be lit up when someone is writing an untruth. In the case of a pathological lie-teller, their brain is not responding in the same way. The brain part that is meant to respond to a lie that is being presented is not as active. They have managed to convince their brains to accept lies as true facts. They believe in truths they store in their minds before they actually state them. They create real memories of these falsehoods as if they really happened. If you can convincing your brain to believe that the lies don't exist and that all you are processing is factual, you're at the same level as an egregious lie-teller.

For an average person who is attempting lying, they would not have the same level of accuracy as an experienced pathological liar. It's because lying consumes far more brain power to be able to tell the truth. When you are honest your brain simply relates to events that have occurred. In contrast in a lie you are trying to build an experience it isn't familiar with and convince itself that it's working with an actual event that took place. If you're trying to create a lie an expert in truth can spot and distinguish your lies from reality before you say anything. Based on these factual statements dealing with a lying person can have two results They could have a good reputation or bad. If they're too good, you could think that they are telling the entire truth, or just a part of it that is mingled with truth. If they're too bad you could conclude they're lying or doing it for fun. As you can see, it's difficult to identify a lying person.

The way to become a truth-seeker or an effective lie detector isn't so evident. You can't rely on a single indicator to spot all the lying people that you meet. To understand this, can you trust a single indicator or cue to determine that someone is interested in you, or likes you? To spot liars we require more than one clue. These are known as statistical cues that deceive. They represent non-verbal and verbal behaviors that are common to liars.

They are able to lie about items that do not be the alarm. If you're able to identify a prolific lie, recognizing a typical lying person will appear to be an unpaid job. Pay attention to these characteristics that could quickly expose an infamous liar.

* This group of people tend to be those with an optimistic view of lying. These individuals believe in the benefits of lying and can be a normal coping strategy in all situations.
If you're looking for gender they are predominantly male. They are typically younger and are proud of their high status in the workplace.
* They're not worried or ashamed of their lying behavior. They are willing to admit that they have told at least 5 every day.
* The victim pool of these individuals is usually their families. They tend to be more likely to lie to their partners and children.
If you compare it to the lying habits of a normal person, the liars who are prolific lie

five times more often than the average person.
* They might be hesitant to lie if it serves their own interests, such as having an unspoken secret that no one else should be able to know. However they may not be able to accept lying if they believe that it could have an adverse effect on those who are close to them.
* For every major lie that is told by a normal person the prolific liars record 19.1 lies. With these characteristics it is evident that a notorious lie-teller is more likely to commit a lie at even a second's notice. They only consider lying if it is beneficial to them , and they will not be honest if they believe that they are putting people near their heart in peril.

#2: Identifying the Nose

We've all heard of the fame and the triumph of Pinocchio. Every lie he told was linked to an uncontrollable expansion of his nose. In spite of the humor that comes with this old tale there is some realness to the actions of one's nose when they're presenting an untruth.

It's an established fact that lying is often associated with having a swollen nose. Neurologists such as Alan Hirsch approve this finding. The reason is that the human nose is a home to the erectile tissues responsible for the nose's sensitivity area. They are responsible for the itchy sensation on the nose. When an average person attempts to lie the erectile tissue will increase blood flow to the area. When the sensitivity of your nose increasing and you'll have only one option: rub or scratch it each time you lie. In this way the Pinocchio story begins to make sense.

It is impossible to conclusively say that everyone who puts their nose in their mouth while giving the speech is lying. There are numerous elements of the environment and climate that can play a role in denying this approach of lying. For instance, due to health issues one could be suffering with a rinsing nose. If this is the scenario, you'll be left with the option of having to frequently contact your nose. Additionally, cold weather or the environment can tend towards making our nostrils itchy. This is also the reason why you may notice yourself scratching at your nose. But, don't dismiss the nose scratching as a way to detect lies. It's a statistical indicator that has yielded reliable results in numerous instances. It is all you need to do is be extremely adept at discerning the individual involved as well as the surroundings around them.

#3 The Neck is Touching

Another non-verbal signal or reaction in response to someone lying is to touch their neck. This approach to detecting lies isn't easy to ignore as is the case with an itchy or irritable nose. The neck is a great spot for detecting deceit and lying. The reasoning behind someone touching their neck when lying is easy. The person will use this method due to being taken to court red handed. If you're found lying on your hands, you'll be more anxious or nervous. Anxiety and nervousness are related to sweating. If you sweat around the neck, you'll feel a sensation of tingling, especially when you wear an earmuff. The discomfort can force you to take off your collar, or rub the neck area until you feel more normal. When you scratch your neck, you'll try to rid yourself of the tingling feeling. The tingling sensation can extend to the tissues of your face, and cause you to constantly wash your face. In the average, this individual is likely to scratch their necks five times if they're caught telling an untruth.

#4: Mismatched Hand Gestures

If you are observing a sincere or sincere individual, the body movements are never off-balance. They'll always match. For instance, in hand gestures, when you accuse a person who is honest with a bad smell, they'll immediately close their mouths and cross their arms or even firmly clench their hands to form an oblique fist. In the case of the liar, their response could be very different. Their body language can trigger the correct reaction, however their hand gestures can act differently. In the majority of situations their hand gestures do not match the body language.

To be a deceiver the hand gesture they make could be towards a different direction than the direction they are looking. It is possible that you are pointing directly toward yourself when your gaze is to the left. A truthful or falsely accused person ensures that their gaze follows the direction of their pointed finger.

If there's a discord between your eyes and the direction you are making your hand movements This could indicate that you aren't able to be able to align the words you're using with reality.

Chapter 13: Hypnotization

Hypnotization involves getting a person's mind into an open-minded state that is completely open to suggestions. A person who is hypnotized can be described as an insomniac whose mind is primarily focused on walking, but completely unaffected by signals that come from the the world.
In that state of hypnotism person who has been hypnotized is unable to make references to sources outside of the body and only draw references from suggestions. The person may be largely or completely loses their peripheral vision.
Hypnotic Induction
Hypnotic induction involves using an initial set of instructions and tips to draw the person into a state of hypnosis. The main characteristics of hypnosis are
* Focused attention to an idea or object
* Isolation from the peripheral view
* Increasing reception to suggestions

Dark contrasts with. White Hypnosis

The distinction between hypnosis that is white and dark is in the intention of the person who is hypnotized. Dark hypnosis is utilized to take advantage of the person who is hypnotized to make a profit for the person who is hypnotized. In the same way white hypnosis can improve the hypnotic experience by helping the hypnotic to snap out of an unforgiving or damaging state of mind.

Hypnotherapy

Hypnotherapy is a type of white hypnotic hypnotherapy that is used by medical professionals to treat patients. The primary goal is to assist patients recover from emotional, psychological physical, emotional and even physical trauma. Hypnotherapy may be utilized in relief from pain to allow the patient to separate himself from the cause of the pain, thereby reducing the pain's sensitivity. The following facts about hypnosis:

It's a choice.
* It's a willful.
The children are much more vulnerable to hypnotism than adults.
* 15 Percent of people are susceptible to hypnotism.
A mere 10% could not be easily attracted.
* Those who find themselves easily caught up in fantasies are more prone to the hypnotism.

Dark Hypnosis
There are numerous victims of dark, inductions to hypnosis. Here are a few of the most common reasons for dark, hypnotic induction
The hypnotist is able to manipulate you in such an degree that you are willing to give everything you own to the one who is hypnotizing.
The trick is to get you seduced in a way that makes you want to open your doors to criminals.
* They were in a state of hypnosis that

made you go with kidnappers to their hideout.

Facts and Fiction, as well as the Psychology that drives it

Hypnosis is, as has been mentioned, the subject of a lot of doubt. However, the current methods of hypnotherapy as well as the utilization of altered states of consciousness for interrogation of prisoners could misrepresent the amount of attention that hypnosis is subject to. The theory of hypnosis is believed to have its roots in the ancient times of Egypt and India where people were advised to heal themselves by spiritual experiences or altered states. By 'temple sleeping' an ancient practice, people were encouraged to sleep in places of worship to reenergize their bodies and minds.

Hypnosis has gone through several variations in modern times, but they're founded on the notion it is possible to control the mind by the trance state or altered states of mind. We'll be examining its history just before it became well-known through Franz Mesmer.

How Mesmer began Mesmerizing

In the time that Franz Mesmer was a young medical student, he was studying under the guidance of a Jesuit monk called Father Maximillian Hell. Hell was an astronomer and researcher who was fascinated with the natural world , and in the workings of solar system as well as the regions that are polar on the earth, and also the human body. Hell began to develop an interest in the use of magnets to enhance the power of healing. He also taught Mesmer, his pupil Mesmer to the art of magnetic therapy.

Mesmer adopted the Hell's method of magnetic therapy. It utilized magnetized rocks to enhance circulation of the fluids within the body. Mesmer developed and expanded their applications. Mesmer often had patients ingest iron shavings and then employ a magnet to draw these shavings into the digestive tract. Mesmer believed that patients might be cured of whatever was wrong with them if they could get their vital fluid back in order.

Mesmer described this technique as early as "animal magnetism," and he believed it was possible to heal people with the magnetic laying of hands. Later, he came up with a more closely related method of hypnosis. This method required sitting closely with the patient, while they held their hands, and often rubbing their shoulders armpits and torsos all while keeping eye contact. After a time, patients would scream and their bad or unhappiness would disappear.

Still skeptical? That was the case for many people that day In 1784, the committee was set up to examine not Mesmer himself, but one his associates, a physician known as d'Eslon who was required to administer Mesmer's treatment with mixed outcomes. Why is this so important? Because the committee investigating discovered that the methods were pseudoscience, and were based on "imagination. However, they did work occasionally and the main issue is: why?

Then for the Next Theory

Mesmer's work was largely dismissed and criticized, Mesmer himself retreated from medical practice, taking a trip around Europe and living in silence until his death in 1815. Then, a few years later, Scottish surgeon James Braid was to believe in Mesmer's work eventually.

Braid was a well-known surgeon and physician who made an innovative treatment for clubfoot as well as other orthopedic problems in the extremities. He was born in 1841. Braid had been invited to an event for healing by Mesmer's former student and an Frenchman known as Charles Lafontaine. Lafontaine permitted doctors to step onto his stage as they used magnetic treatment and examined his patients.

Braid was one of the doctors who did so and observed that all of them appeared to be in a state or altered mental state. Although

Braid was previously not convinced that magnetism was a legitimate medical procedure and was so enthralled that he kept attending the healing demonstrations of Lafontaine until he had an understanding of how the treatments could be effective. One thing he observed consistently was that patients appeared to be awake in the middle of sleep.'

After some reflection Braid came to the conclusion that the altered state of the patients was caused by the magnets of Lafontaine, but rather his behavior. The magnetist's actions triggered the altered state, which Braid named neuro-hypnosis, which is the Greek for "nervous sleep". Braid began to experiment with the method at home to determine whether he could induce the state himself. He concluded that a state of hypnosis can be induced through ocular or visual fixation. The research also disproved the concept of magnets being used in the Lafontaine's treatment.

Braid introduced the concept of hypnotism

being a psycho-physiological phenomenon in late 1841 to mixed reactions among the academic community. In his first presentation, Braid demonstrated that he could induce the same sleepy state of mind as Lafontaine however without the magnets. While Braid was a target of many critics who were adamant that people could heal through suggestion, he went further to incorporate hypnotism into its medical practices as a possible alternative, or added treatment to the alleviation of pain , as well as other physical and mental ailments.

CHAPTER 14: HOW TO GUARD YOURSELF FROM MANIPULATORS

How to speed-read people and prevent Manipulation

Speed-reading takes time and practice. However, a lot of the skills you will need to master could be abilities you already possess. When you examine an individual to bring the person in your head you're looking at the way they look in a single second. You are able to see the expression of their face as well as their posture and their movements.

To be able to speed read people efficiently To do this, you must be knowledgeable about meditation. Mindfulness means being aware of the present moment, without judgment and is a set-up consisting of three elements that include being present, present in the present moment, and being non-judgmental. The first one, being aware, is simply taking in all the sensory information that you can and being aware of the state of your being. The second is about staying in the present moment, no matter where and when you are. The third section is about not judging. This is applicable to those who tend to get lost in their own thoughts. The importance of non-judging is that acceptance is an important motivator for us all. It is essential to cultivate mindfulness in order to be able to read people quickly because it's the way that you'll be comfortable reading people's signals and other signals.

Get started on developing mindfulness by practicing. The first step is to lie down in a comfortable place and let your body relax and letting your body feel your butts in the chair, and put your feet down on the ground. There are a number of exercises, such as the body scan. Body scans should begin at the one end of your body, such as the toes or head, and then move slowly towards the opposite end to the back. This is simply focussing your attention on different areas of your body, taking note of the things they're doing and what's happening. Concentrate your attention on your toesand be aware of what they feel. It is possible to feel the clothing you are touching the socks or shoes and even feel the surface underneath the feet. This allows you to become more aware of what's happening in your body.

You could also begin simply by being aware of the breath. Focus your attention to the physical sensations that accompany the breath. It's a way to be in tune with the body and connect with it. As you take note of each breath, count up to 10 repeatedly. Check how far you can go without losing focus to a single body task. This exercise will aid in focusing and focus.

Mindfulness lets you stay in the present moment while you are in contact with people and looking at them. Being mindful is being conscious, and that is the goal you should aim for when trying to read people at a faster speed. You must be conscious of their the way they talk, along with other clues which are crucial when analyzing individuals.

Attention and concentration are crucial when you are trying to read fast. It is necessary to focus your focus and focus on an individual when you're speed reading them. It is not necessary to seem to be focusing all your attention on them, but instead watching them. You should first notice their posture. Are they sitting straight? Are they seated or leaning towards one side? This could indicate the physical condition and posture of the body. The older people have a slight hunched-over viewpoint. For younger people an hunch could refer to various things. It could be that they'd like to appear smaller and less noticeable. Perhaps they aren't a fan of being out in the open. It could indicate a feeling of shyness within them and that they're unwilling to stand and stare people in the eyes.

The posture of people's bodies can reveal a lot about them, too. People who are extremely aware try to keep a good posture all the time, since bad posture can cause bones to break down and result in a variety of health issues. If you see someone sitting in an upright and healthy posture, you will know that they're a reliable individual. They are mindful of their bodies and take care of their bodies. Sometimes, a sitting position may not be the most reliable indicator of health, and it is possible that it can cause confusion.

What is an the term "effect? The term "effect" refers to the manner that your face communicates emotions and thoughts. A normal expression is to be one with a range of facial expressions, such as smiling when smiling and showing facial expressions that correspond to the words one is doing. The way one appears is a major indicator of the way someone feels. Patients with mental illness are, for instance, characterized by unchanging effects. The result is that their behavior doesn't change much when they speak different words and are unable to express their feelings through their eyes. This can be caused by a variety of circumstances. However, less severe instances of restricted effects can be due to being shy, anxious or depressed. One may limit their effects when they suffer from anxiety about social situations, for instance. People's thoughts could be in a tizzy state across the room and their facial expression displayed as a calm, neutral attitude. This is a defensive strategy for certain people, when they are unable to express their feelings. The rest of us do not have to confront the grim reality of what your feelings are. Certain people express all their emotions in their appearances. When you are speed reading someone you only need to figure out the extent to which a person's expression conveys their mood. After that, you are able to connect with them. Eye contact is an important component of this. What amount of eye contact is the individual making? Do they have a steady and intimate relationship? Do you think it's broken apart? Sometimes, people may be insecure with eye contact or eye contact. It can also be a method for people to show their power in a particular situation.

Contact with the eyes is common factor that connects and also divide people. "Old-fashioned "male gaze" was coined to refer to the relationship that occurs with eyes or gaze by itself. The male gaze is a result of the strength of the eyes. This is something is often forgotten, but eye contact is an effective instrument when you are making contact with an individual. It is a way to establish a bond. This can be a scary experience for some as well as those that are timid or suffer from issues with self-esteem tend towards avoiding eye contact a large degree. This is due to the fact that they aren't confident in themselves and don't feel confident. Confident people is able to look at any person they meet and interact with. Some people can be intimidating but you'll be able to be in good faith and possess the confidence to present your thoughts and ideas clearly.

One way you can begin with speed reading is by doing a lot of practice. Get some practice in at the corner store and purchase something small or two. Take a look around and observe whom you can spot. If you don't see anyone else, try working with the cashier. Ask them about their day and observe what they respond to. While traversing this process make sure to take in the most you can. Focus on them without distraction in the background, and try to read the body language and their impact. You may be able to notice something you've never seen before.

Once you're back home, you can begin writing. Write down what you observed how the person looked like, the way they behaved and so on. Begin to write about the way you felt inside your body while in contact with the person, and look to see if your body changed in your body when you were with them. The most important things to look at are eyes, face expressions body language, facial expressions, and any other nuances that you might sense. Begin to write down every thing you observe and note what you can learn from it.

CHAPTER 15 THE MASTER OF YOUR OWN EMOTIONS

Many of the actions that we do are influenced by emotions. What we say, how we think about, what we feel and what we do as a result of those emotions. Every single one of these is caused by this strong emotional, volatile force in us that we have a lot of trouble controlling. Only those who have the highest levels of emotional intelligence have managed to overcome their emotions, ensuring they are in control regardless of the situation they're in, by learning to manage their emotions.

They won't openly admit that they're experiencing emotions However, you can observe the emotion written on their face and body language.

Body language can be seen throughout the day and is a major indication that someone could feel an intense emotion is how they express themselves. Faces, like we've already established is always the first place you interact with. Adults are able to cover their emotions in the best way they can most often, particularly when they are in an office environment.

Sometimes, it's not however, and If you're paying attention you'll be able to see the variety of emotions displayed by those all around you.

In a day, one person can go through several emotions as the day progresses--everything from stress, anger, happiness, joy, jubilation, exhilaration, enthusiasm, and more.

In addition to analyzing body language for indications of the emotions that a person could be feeling, additional areas to be observed include:

* General behavior
* Mannerisms
• Tone and voice
* Deed
• Physical Health (when certain emotions are experienced at a high and extreme degree such as anxiety or depression the symptoms manifest physically)

THE EMOTIONAL SIGNS

As we've discussed in previous chapters, certain emotions are more obvious than others , because they're so obvious that it's impossible to ignore them even in the event of trying. Certain emotions are so obvious that it's impossible to mistake them as any other emotion. They are the primary emotions we experience that we experience the frequently and widely.

Let's take a look at some of these easy-to-identify emotions:

EMOTION 1 - HAPPINESS

The feeling everyone strives for. If you ask anyone what they would like and they'll say they'd like to be content. Even with all the other demands wishes, desires, and wants under the surface everyone is looking to be content. If someone is joyous, joyful or full of joy there are signs that are difficult to miss.

They'll be smiling a lot for one reason and it's nearly impossible to erase the smile from their faces. They exude passion, talk with passion Their body language and gestures are friendly and warm. Their attitude is so positive that you're sure to be happy in their presence.

2. EMOTION - SADNESS

Sadness is a powerful emotion that's difficult to conceal. It's so strong that people can detect that you're suffering simply when they look at your even before you've even spoken any words. The sadness will show in your eyesand face, or perhaps your arms crossed over your chest, your shoulders in a hunch and your gaze orientated towards the downwards, which indicates your unhappiness.

When someone is unsatisfied, and is in a conversation with you their feet and upper body will usually be set in a different direction from the conversation, signalling their desire to stop the conversation since their mind is focused elsewhere.

3. EMOTION 3 - ANGER

There's no denying anger when you look at it. It's, perhaps one of the most straightforward emotions to spot following happiness. It's usually associated with a very clear body expressions. A deep frown, eyes tightly pressed together with lips that are tight and thin and tense, fists that are rolled up and tense shoulders, nostrils flaring with clenched jaws and muscles are all indicators how angry is the predominant emotion that a person is feeling. The tone of voice they speak with will be harsh and have an anger-filled edge that is clear what they are feeling.

#4 - FEAR

In all the emotions we can experience the fear emotion is our most fundamental emotion. This is the emotion responsible for triggering the "fight or flight" response which is in each of us. Again, this feeling is simple to recognize. The expression on the face and body language can be an obvious sign that someone is afraid.

The eyes of the victim will be large, they are scared or their mouths may opened in the fear or in surprise, their lips are trembling and nostrils tense, they may even get cold sweats. They usually begin across the face.

5th EMOTION - SURPRISE

Of all the five emotion types, this is the one that lasts the longest. The feeling of surprise is brief and fleeting typically only several minutes, and sometimes even a few seconds. The feeling of surprise occurs when confronted by something new and the physiological reaction that usually follows is the shock reaction. Contrary to the other emotions surprise can be either pleasant or negative.

The 5 primary emotions

A delightful surprise could be the moment your friends and family present you with an unexpected birthday celebration. Unpleasant surprises happen when who scares or jumps on you. Because surprise can catch us by surprise, it also creates an adrenaline rush that triggers our fight-or-flight response.

EXPERIENCE MANIPULATION BY RECORDING YOUR EM THE MANIPULATION

I'm fine. This is the most commonly-told lie that is told. The use of deceit and manipulation has become so widespread that everybody has been victimized or the victim at one point or another. You've been either lied to or made up lies. You've been tricked or have done the deceiving. You've been deceived or you're the one who is manipulating. But there are some lies that are not intended to trick you. For instance, if someone says "I'm fine," don't be concerned', and they're not It could be their way of stopping you from asking questions, because they don't want to talk about it at the moment.

The indicators of deceit are evident once you know what you're seeking. One indication (aside of the body language) that deceit could be occurring is when people are prone to sidetrack the questions they are asked with lengthy inexplicably lengthy explanations. Lies, manipulators, and deceivers are throughout the place you visit. They may be present in your circle of friends or even within your family.

While they may appear to seem as individuals some aspects that manipulators share in common one of which is that they're deceitful, sneaky as well as apathetic, and they'll employ any strategy to get their desired outcome at at the end. They are not concerned about your feelings, or anyone else's and even those they love. They will not hesitate to use your feelings against you. If you're not able to exercise any control over your feelings, you're an easy victim. All that matters is their goals and the results they're seeking.

The oldest method of manipulation that exists. Anyone who is trying to influence or gain advantage from someone else will employ this method to gain or even thrive and take satisfaction in knowing that they've pulled you off of your feet. A skilled manipulator and liar can manipulate with such a subtle manner and if you're not skilled in reading body language you'll not be able to tell what's going on till it's already too late, and you've either been misled or misled. The purpose of lying is to gain the trust of other people. They use manipulation to hide their true motives.

They use lies to get an inch ahead competitors.

The deceit and manipulation is everywhere in every aspect of your life, including at workplace. Someone who was worried regarding their job could contact the boss to inquire whether they're likely to be dismissed or laid off. The boss might attempt to conceal what's happening to avoid putting a strain on the work that needs to be completed by tricking the employee into thinking that there is nothing going on, and reassure that everything is good and there's nothing else to be concerned about. While knowing that it's not true. A coworker who's been looking for the same job that you are could hide information in order to make themselves more attractive to you. The parents who would like their children to be free to do whatever they like might resort to manipulative strategies to force them to obey the guidelines.

Manipulators are often highly emotional people, who are prone to extreme or even hysterical eruptions when they wish things to go in their preferred way. If you're not the one who controls your emotional state, you can easily become caught up in the time and be as emotional. It's so intense, in fact so much that it begins to impair your judgement and prevents your ability to think clearly. The most damaging part is that they play with your emotions , playing the role of a friend earning your trust in order to collect data that they can make use of against you in the future.

Why do I need to Learn to Master My EMOTIONS?

If you aren't in control of your emotions, you'll be able to exercise limited control over many different aspects in your daily life. You can react in a way that is inappropriate when your emotions aren't controlled, and you are prone to say or do things that aren't right. You become agitated over the smallest of issues which makes it difficult for other people to interact with you.

You can become volatile and susceptible to mood swings. This affects your behavior and your character as an individual. If you're labeled one with a personality disorder, or "overly emotional" and people begin to avoid them and making excuses for not to join your group.

In the end, not having control over your emotions can make you a prime to be a target. A shrewd manipulator is able to determine the buttons to push to can get you excited enough to play with your emotions to force the victim into doing things that would normally not do. If you don't develop the skills to manage emotional states, your feelings (and the manipulators that surround you) will be your sole masters.

Indicates that you're being MANIPULATED

We're constantly trying to influence one another by some way, or inviting acquaintances to try a brand new product you've enjoyed because you love it. You're sharing thoughts and trying to influence people to look at things from your perspective and the reason why your strategy should be one that others share your thoughts and video content via social media in order to influence other people to join in with your views.

Managers, supervisors, leaders and bosses influence the people under their supervision and encourage them to pursue the same objective. Marketers and advertisers attempt to convince customers of purchasing products and services by the variety of advertisements and marketing campaigns they launch.

If influence happens constantly When does it become clear that there is a line between influence to manipulative?

What is the difference between manipulation and influence or persuasion?

Doesn't manipulating, persuasion or influence basically the identical?

You're trying to convince someone else to join or be with you?

Persuasion, manipulation, and influence are similar but they have different names. One characteristic that distinguishes manipulation from other two. It is the intent. Manipulation can be ruthless and devious and will always result in one person being taken advantage of or abused. Influence and persuasion are not as ruthless or cunning. The manipulation is done to gain a profit and only benefit the person who is manipulating.

Manipulators force others to perform their will by threatening and pressure. The motivation in your behavior is the thing that differentiates influence and persuasion from manipulation. Sincere intentions and a determination to create an environment which benefits the other person is the essence of influence and persuasion. If you're determined to be a good person, this is persuasion. If you're sincere from the beginning regarding what you're attempting to accomplish, then that's persuasion.

If you are able to affirm with conviction that you are in the best interests of your partner in mind, that's persuasion.

Manipulators do not care about anyone other than their own. There's only one thing in their heads and it's focused on them, their wants and desires, as well as what's best for them. If they can get what they would like, they do not care whether they hurt themselves in the process. If they need to get over your feet to reach the top and they'll do it. If they have to stab at you with a knife to reach the top the mountain, they'll take it on. They aren't concerned what the implications of their decisions. They only want to get their way.

Manipulation is everywhere and you may be an innocent victim while you read this. The first sign that you may be the victim of manipulative behavior is when you notice that something's not quite right in a relationship you're in. It's difficult to identify the issue but having that person around never makes you feel happy. Even when you're with your family and friends Instead of feeling content when you spend your time around them you're becoming more stressed, annoyed or confused than when you first began.

Perhaps it's the coworker at work who constantly tries to entice to make you do their will even though it was your intention to say no at the beginning. There's a reason why you are embarrassed to not help them even though you've the right to refuse since you've got a lot to manage. This could be a sign that you're in the midst of an opportunist.

Manipulation can occur in a variety of ways. It can range in the world of dealing with an aggressive and exigent person to being in a relationship an unfaithful partner. Certain manipulative traits are easier to recognize, while others are carefully concealed to create the impression that this type of behaviour will be "normal".

If you suspect something is amiss take a look with your gut and watch for warning signs below to indicate you may be a victim of manipulative tactics:

Always Your Own Fault A typical sign of manipulation is that, regardless of what you do or say in the end, it's your blame. Even when it's notyour fault, even if you've never done anything wrong, are you the person to blame? What's the mechanism behind that? The manipulator is skilled at rearranging and transforming facts to suit the circumstances. You're an easy to target. The one friend who has always some excuse to justify their poor behaviour or bad judgement The one who constantly gives you the blame is not a friend. You're manipulative. I wouldn't have done that in the event that you believed that it was a mistake. I appreciate it and now take a look at the things you've done! What's the reason you didn't stop me? The hallmark characteristic of manipulative "friend" is that somehow you're always in the middle and are is made to feel as if you're being manipulated.

* Forced Agreeability- Do you find yourself being forced into doing something you do not want to do because the person who made your request make you feel uneasy for saying"no? Feeling constantly guilty, pressured or pressured into agreeing even if it's from someone else, isn't usual behaviour. It's manipulative, and they're playing with your guilt to gain advantage.

And if you're scared to say "no," this is a signal that something in this relationship isn't correct. Not at all. It is not a good idea to feel as if you're being threatened or pressured to sign a contract however, if you do not develop the ability to control the emotions of your mind, an opportunist can quickly profit and make you feel the most guilty they can.

"Insecurity" You're confident in your decision just five minutes ago. When you got to the person in your family or friend And suddenly, you're not sure anymore. Five moments ago, you seemed certain and confident, but today that same decision is filling you with doubt, leading you to doubt your judgement. After that single encounter. Do you recognize this? If yes, then you could have to face the reality that it's someone in your family, friend, or coworker that is manipulative. If you spend enough time around them and they'll make you feel like a failure or like you're a complete loss, and that whatever you do won't ever be a good idea. Discuss any idea, thought or thought and they'll figure out an opportunity to alter it to the point of making it appear like something that's not even worth thinking about.

www.ingramcontent.com/pod-product-compliance
Lightning Source LLC
Chambersburg PA
CBHW071838080526
44589CB00012B/1045